The
TEA LOVER'S
Companion

Also by James Norwood Pratt

The Wine Bibber's Bible
The Tea Lover's Treasury

The
TEA LOVER'S
Companion

The Ultimate Connoisseur's Guide to
Buying, Brewing, and Enjoying Tea

JAMES NORWOOD PRATT
WITH DIANA ROSEN

A BIRCH LANE PRESS BOOK
PUBLISHED BY CAROL PUBLISHING GROUP

"The Total Abstainer" by M. F. K. Fisher, copyright © 1982 M. F. K. Fisher,
originally appeared in *The New Yorker*. Reprinted by permission.

A Birch Lane Press Book
Published by Carol Publishing Group
Birch Lane Press is a registered trademark of
Carol Communications, Inc.
Editorial Offices: 600 Madison Avenue, New York, N.Y. 10022
Sales and Distribution Offices: 120 Enterprise Avenue, Secaucus,
N.J. 07094
In Canada: Canadian Manda Group, One Atlantic Avenue, Suite 105,
Toronto, Ontario M6K 3E7
Queries regarding rights and permissions should be addressed to
Carol Publishing Group, 600 Madison Avenue, New York, N.Y. 10022

Carol Publishing Group books are available at special discounts for
bulk purchases, sales promotion, fund-raising, or educational
purposes. Special editions can be created to specifications. For
details, contact: Special Sales Department, Carol Publishing
Group, 120 Enterprise Avenue, Secaucus, N.J. 07094

Manufactured in the United States of America
10 9 8 7 6 5 4 3 2 1

Library of Congress Cataloging-in-Publication Data
Pratt, James Norwood.
    The tea lover's companion : the ultimate connoisseur's guide to
buying, brewing, and enjoying tea / James Norwood Pratt with Diana
Rosen
        p.   cm.
    "A Birch Lane Press book."
    ISBN 1-55972-323-8 (hc)
    1. Tea. I. Rosen, Diana. II. Title.
TX817.T3P73   1995
641.3'372—dc20   95-19228
                                                            CIP

To my sons,
John Norwood Davis Pratt and Rowell Aleister Sterling Pratt
"non generant aquilae columbas"
with abiding love

Contents

PART 3

PREFACE

$\mathcal{P}$leasure is far too serious to take lightly. If you find this truth self-evident, you are one of those for whom the world's fine teas are intended. We are all perfectly competent to judge what pleases us in entertainment, food and drink. Once you have drunk enough teas to have a preference for some—and perhaps a distaste for others—you are already on the road to connoisseurship: It's not a word to attach too much importance to. As a practice, on the other hand, it can be the source of pleasure for a lifetime. It is a way to focus, to center. In a world constantly telling you to hurry up, it is the easiest way to slow down.

Tea is the constant companion of my days, sometimes stimulating, sometimes soothing, sometimes a sociable interlude with others, sometimes a comforting solace. Mornings it means a strong black tea in my case, drunk from an old-fashioned, outsized "breakfast cup" I treasure for the purpose. Today's was a peppery China Yunnan, and then a high-grown Ceylon from Nuwara Eliya with flavors as deep as organ notes, faintly sweet and woody. I don't always feel like a second pot—indeed, I don't always feel like either of these teas. I might choose a Ceylon from several other regions. Sometimes it's a malty Assam I want, or an incomparable Keemun. All of these are good with milk and sugar, which is how I like my eye-openers best.

Writing till mid-morning generally makes me thirsty for a green tea, appetizingly bitter and astringent. I take my time choosing which I'll prepare in the traditional Chinese way, that is, to be brewed in and sipped from a *guywan*, Mandarin for "covered cup." Today I settled on Liuan Guapian, deservedly one of China's ten most famous teas. Drinking tea this way allows me to make cup after aromatic cup from the same leaf simply by replenishing the hot water. Eventually I notice the flavor has begun to fade, and know it's time for lunch.

Lunchtime iced tea—a major food group for us Southerners—calls for no comment as long as it's wet and goes down the right way. Once back at my desk, however, I'm ready for something wonderful as a postprandial digestif and pick-me-up. Today it was a delicate and magnificently flowery Darjeeling from the Namring estate's second crop, or "flush." I like Darjeelings made Chinese-style too, but today I prepared a small pot instead, steeping it exactly three minutes and drinking it neat, as God intends Darjeeling to be taken. The aftertaste lingered a full half hour after the last swallow. With the shank of the afternoon came time for the most difficult choice of my tea day: what to serve the guests expected at four o'clock.

The habit inherited from my Anglo-Saxon ancestors is to offset that "sinking feeling" in late afternoon with black tea like Nilgiri or some other, small matter which, as long as it's fragrant and hearty, goes well with food and takes to milk and sugar. But not today. However dear English-style afternoon tea may remain, I now know many other kinds of tea fit for the purpose and other ways of making them. Today's mood was for dry biscuits, fruits and nuts—salty cashews and Medjool dates—with an extraordinary China oolong, Monkey-Picked Ti Kuan Yin, prepared kung-fu-style. As hoped, my friends were intrigued with the Taiwanese fist-sized kung-fu teapot and thimble cups and could not get enough of the tea, powerfully aromatic, deep-flavored and strong as original sin. The buzz it produced made us talky and animated, and no tea-making ceremony seems to produce greater relaxation or intimacy.

Darjeeling is perfect for after dinner and is easily decaffeinated when need be. Tonight, however, I have treated myself to a solitary *guywan* of Dragon Well, another species of greatness, my reigning favorite amongst all the world's green teas. The spirit of China inhabits its nectar. I shall enjoy its luscious, vegetative companionship for several more infusions, looking up from these sentences at the fog blanketing San Francisco Bay and pausing to listen to foghorns. Before bedtime, as always, I'll have a cup of China's ancient Pu-Er tea, as healthful as anything doctors know how to prescribe, and I will sleep soundly. Whatever else tomorrow holds, it will assuredly include tea—though which tea, exactly, I won't know till then.

There you have it—"a hardened and shameless tea drinker." Simply buying this book may put you at risk of becoming a fellow addict. You will find in the infusion of this fascinating plant both social lubricant and private comfort, restoring and nourishing body and spirit with a sense of well-being nothing else provides. (To its effects I think I may attribute much of my health and most of my good cheer.) You should not be surprised if such an insidious pleasure becomes a passion with you.

Tea is quiet. Its taste is subtler than wine, though there's just as much to discover in it if your palate is also quiet and attentive. The range of types and flavors is just as wide also—the white, red, and rose categories of wine have their parallels in green, black, and oolong teas. Pu-Er might even be likened to fortified wines, and white tea compared to unfermented grape must. And any one of these may come from literally hundreds of different growing regions, each with its specific plant types, soil, elevation and climate. However much you learn, you will never know all there is to know about it, and that is part of tea's charm and its mystery.

Reading is a damnably poor substitute for experience when it comes to developing an appreciation for tea. Think of it as a way of sharpening the senses, of cultivating your taste. Although a liking for tea can come with the first cup, you come to understand and appreciate it more and more with time and experience. Like any other esthetic creation, like music, painting, cooking or poetry, the more you come to know about tea, the more you find in it to enjoy. It can take you lands away, and into many different times and cultures.

The taste of tea is only one of the pleasures it affords. It brightens the spirits and makes us feel good. It is a way of relaxing that leads to conversation or else contemplation and dreams. It fosters a love for beautiful things to handle and look at. However prepared, tea requires a certain amount of ceremony, which most of us miss without even realizing we lack it. It soothes the heart.

There are dozens of different ceremonies, different ways to make and enjoy tea. Each of them inculcates civility, not only in relation to others and in the respect due the humble leaf itself, this curious product of the earth and human hands. And just as tea alters consciousness, exploring its history and ways can alter our understanding of history and humankind. This is what has happened to me as my horizons were gradually broadened by exploring the history of a drink as ancient as the pyramids. It is a story which transports you by Russian caravan and clipper ships, one which leads from botany to Buddhism and the economics of the British raj, from saints to Chinese emperors and American revolutionaries, omitting a very great deal else. And through tea, you may become friends with some of our most fascinating contemporaries, the men and women who love it.

At its simplest, tea requires no special equipment—just hot water and a container in which to brew the leaf. On the other hand, it can get rather complicated, like wine, with a multitude of special accoutrements to enhance the delight. This is because tea is not just a product, it is a practice, what the Asian sages call a "Way." It is the opposite of otherworldly, however, for the Way begins with appreciating what is in the cup before us. And here we have literally a world of choices. The purpose of this book is to make them available to you.

—James Norwood Pratt

ACKNOWLEDGMENTS

Special thanks are due my generous friends and teachers Grace and Roy Fong of Imperial Tea Court, who have initiated me into the mysteries of China tea. For kindness, interest and friendship I am again indebted to Mr. Richard Sanders of Grace Rare Tea, Karen and Augie Techiera of Freed Teller & Freed, and Mr. Michael Spillane of G. S. Haly Company. These were my first teachers in tea, and they haven't given up on me yet.

My gratitude also extends to many tea friends in India, China, Europe and the United States, among others Mr. Devan Shah of India Tea Importers, Mr. Madhavan Nambiar, former director of the Tea Board of India, Professor Chen Zhong-mao, director of the Tea Research Institute, Hangzhou, Mr. John C. Evans, author of *Tea in China*, Mrs. Helen Gustafson of Chez Panisse, Miss Mary O'Brien of Chaiwalla and Messrs. John Harney, Samuel Twining, OPE, and Gaetano Kazuo Maida.

I have benefited greatly from the specialized knowledge of tea and health found in *All the Tea in China* by Kit Chow and Ione Kramer and would like to thank my editor, the inimitable Miss Diana Rosen, for her invaluable assistance.

—JNP

Only a poet, like John Donne, could have thought up a concept that "no man is an island." That goes for the writer herself who may often think she's penning in a vacuum. She soon finds out that the way to the pressroom is via a group of editors, consultants and true friends who challenge, question and soothe the wearied brow all the while supporting her effort. My thanks to editor Marcy Swingle and agent Bill Birnes; The Writer's Computer Store of Sausalito; Daniel Miller and Diane Kordick; Joni Prittie, Karen Strange, Sandy Parry, and to all my tea "buddies" and lovers of the leaf: purveyors Roy and Grace Fong, John and Michael Harney, Joan and Jim Harron, David Lee Hoffman, Devan Shah, Michael J. Spillane and eternally to Richard Sanders for introducing me to James Norwood Pratt.

—DR

THE TOTAL ABSTAINER

Tea—the good old tea that has long been thought to "cheer but not inebriate"—is one of the true refinements of our present culture, and I am always ready to join any discussion that proposes to illuminate its position. Yet, when I write or read about tea, I feel six years old again, or a sullen fourteen. I see my mother sitting like a full-breasted swan behind the Dresden teapot that was always used at lunch; I am carried far away by the perfumes of black and green and amber infusions. But all along I know my humbuggery in daring to recall them, because the cold truth is that I have not tasted even a drop of tea, whether from a Dresden spout or a drugstore tea bag, for more than forty years.

Perhaps this confession, though, will help to clarify my continuing, though vicarious, love of the brew. If I need an excuse, I turn to George Saintsbury, who wrote the small classic called *Notes on a Cellar-Book*, although he himself could not touch wine for the last decades of his life. Tea makes me drunk, or, as I usually think more coldly of it, "drunk as a skunk." I doubt if it has anything to do with my liver—Mr. Saintsbury's was *his* reason for total abstinence—but certainly the chemistry of my body has dictated my sad loss of enjoyment. I found this out after what seemed to me at the time (I was then almost thirty!) a long life of true pleasure with teas, properly brewed.

Before my astonishing penance began, I first drank tea at lunch, when I was between five and eleven. Father came home at noon from his local daily newspaper in Whittier, California, and we all sat down when he did; we ate and talked and smiled when he did, too. And Bertha—or whoever was in the kitchen—brought a tall teapot of Dresden china and its matching cups and so on and put them in front of Mother, at the other end of the quiet but amiable table. We discussed love, money, and politics after dinner but never in the middle of the day, largely because the *News* did not go to press until three, and this was Father's meal, easy-like.

There were often replacements in our kitchen, but we liked Bertha the best, because nobody ever knew whether a platter or even a teacup would reach its goal, thanks to what Mother generally referred to as "shyness" but what we knew was a compulsive tremble directly dictated by Father's mood. Rarely, he would give a bark of laughter at Bertha's palsied reactions to his apparent machismo, and she would weep silently in the kitchen, but mostly we simply sat in suppressed but oddly enjoyable nervousness as she twitched and jittered anxiously around the dining-room table. We loved her, and knew that if she was ever needed, when another domestic accident sent one of our maids-of-the-moment off to jail or to the local asylum, she would be there—shy and shaky, and our friend.

There was always a pot of good cool milk at lunch for my little sister Anne and me, because although Bertha served us just as shakily as she did Grandmother and our parents and anyone else there, we alone drank cambric.

Does anyone talk now about cambric tea? It has undoubtedly been part of all sorts of cosmic finaglings, like the China Trade and other shapings-of-nations, from the nursery on to well-earned serenity and old age. A good cambric recipe calls for one part strong tea in the bottom of a pretty cup or mug and eight to ten parts fine fresh milk, to be stirred by recipient with perhaps a little sugar or honey and, of course, politeness. Cambric tea, as I drank it at lunchtime when I was little, was a privilege, and therefore lapped up like nectar. It made Anne and me feel almost accepted as people, this cool sop to our nascent self-images. The grownups drank their tea hot and dark, as we knew that someday we would, too, and meanwhile our special brew was a fine way to practice.

Grandmother, born in County Tyrone, believed as a good Irishwoman that there were only three kinds of tea fit to drink, none of them to be found among a shop's supplies. The first quality was kept, sensibly enough, in China. The second picking was sent directly to Ireland. The third and lowest grade went, of course, to the benighted British. And all the tea used in our house came once a year, in one or two beautiful soldered tin boxes, from Dublin. Then only would we know it to be second to what the Empress Dowager of China drank, while the Old Lady in Buckingham Palace sipped the dregs, as served her right.

Grandmother also believed that tea, when properly made, should be served strong enough to trot a mouse on. I never tasted her noontime tipple but I feel sure that it was as bitter as it was black, beyond much help from milk or even sugar. I knew, though, that it made cheeks pink and tongues looser as its potency warmed my parents' blood, and I enjoyed their innocent release.

Afternoon Tea was another matter. This was served to guests who came while Grandmother napped, for I suspect that, aside from her innate protest against any notably English customs, her fifty years on the Iowa prairies had dimmed whatever teatime habits she might have retained. This was not true of Mother, though, and after Grandmother died, when I was about twelve, tea was served every day at four o'clock, instead of at the lunch table. Father was never there, but there was always somebody to share it, in our warm, dim living room at the family ranch outside Whittier, and I was increasingly on hand to produce it, releasing our current slavey to catch a bit of rest before dinner was served, promptly at six. Father must be off by seven, to cover the Chamber of Commerce or school supervisors or flood-control meetings for the next day's paper. Sometimes the cook and her boyfriend would want to catch a ride uptown to the movies. Dinner, in other words, was hurried and perfunctory, if always polite, which may explain some of my mother's sensuous enjoyment of Afternoon Tea, as well as my growing resentment of it.

The truth is that I was a pushover, a patsy, for any kind of slavish house jobs so long as I was assured at least weekly that nobody could churn butter on Saturdays as deftly and cleverly and neatly as I, or pick prettier posies, or make nicer tea. For several years, I battened on this sly exploitation. By the time I was well into adolescence, though, I began to see where such flattery had landed me, and I began a long, silent emotional summer. Why was I always the one who had to come in early from playing one o' cat with the kids on the neighboring ranches, or miss a meeting of the Latin Club, to perform the simple but demanding rituals of making tea for a few old ladies? I knew that I would keep on, because I loved Mother and enjoyed pleasing her, but it shamed me to realize my dangerous hunger for recognition. Of course I kept on with the pesky ceremony, and fawned for more praise by baking dainty little cakes and slicing bread the right thinness for nasturtium-leaf sandwiches. As I look back on this silently snarling servitude, I think that I even grew the nasturtiums with Afternoon Tea in mind. It was not admirable, but it was fun, like scratching an old mosquito bite.

There were several teapots at home. I liked the one we always used for lunch when Grandmother was alive: tall, graceful, with little rosebuds here and there on it, and cups and saucers and cream pitcher and hot-water jug to match. There was a slop bowl, of course, for the dregs of cups before fresh tea was poured. Then for two or three people, or Mother and me alone, there was the little Georgian silver set. And if duty called loudly enough to invite the members of the St. Matthias Ladies' Guild, there was the ugly big tea set that had been given to one of the Irish uncles when he was Lord Mayor or something. It was handsome and heavy, very Teutonic, not of sterling silver, and usually Mother kept it out of sight.

My favorite was the little Georgian set. It was lovely to touch, and it meant that only a couple of friends might be there by the glowing fireplace, to murmur over their scones and throw an occasional kind compliment toward me. I never joined them, but grew deft at whisking things on and off the low tea table set by Mother's couch.

Cups and their saucers were pure pleasure from the start, and Mother taught me without words that beautiful objects are made to be used. So that even with palsied Bertha serving lunch, and an occasional wince when a full cup would jig off its saucer before it got down the table to Father, we always used fine Dresden, or Spode, or Sèvres. Or even Chinese porcelain, designed for the Anglo-Saxon tea trade.

In the glassed-in corner cupboard, there was an almost full set of Belleek, sent as a wedding present to Mother. My sister and I stared sometimes at the pale porcelain shells that formed it. Who could ever keep the dust from going in and in, like sand?

As I remember, the Belleek was used only once, when its Irish donors, rich, titled linen weavers, came to explore the Wild West, and stopped to see how we managed afternoon tea there. The whole enterprise was a disaster, mostly because the shell-shaped cups, fairylike in their transparent delicacy, kept tipping over on their three little legs made of tinier rosy or pale-green spiral shells. The pot, a large one on three more substantial but still inadequate rosy shells, turned over. The milk and the sugar spilled. The only thing that stayed upright was the slop bowl, empty because all the tea was here and there on people's knees and laps. And that day's cook had tried to follow a recipe for the biscuits called Slim Johns as made in an Irish castle where Mother had once stayed, and they were burned black, inedible.

After the visitors left, Mother washed the fragile shells herself and put them back in the glassed-in cupboard. We never knew whether there was any sand in all the tiny whorls, but we often looked up respectfully at the pieces, and long after our mother had died Anne sold the set of Belleek to a stylish auctioneer for a startlingly fat sum.

In kitchen cupboards, there were always a few clumsy thick cups with deep saucers, which we never used. I still have one of them, for special guests. It was made for Irishmen, Grandmother said, by the same Chinese who sent us their next-to-the-best tea. That was in the days when one was invited to have a *dish* of tea. The brew was poured into the cup to cool, and then it was poured into the deep saucer and drunk from there. I liked the uncouth romance of all this, and read sometimes in British novels about a "dish o' tea," usually drunk by the lower-class characters.

This old usage recalls another—one that appears occasionally in popular English novels of the nineteen-twenties by Mrs. Belloc Lowndes and others. Somewhere in my reading, for instance, a Kindly Old Country Doctor comes unexpectedly to the lawn where a lady is resting beside the little tea table that a companion has trundled out to her chair. The lady has recently been cleared of killing her husband, by adding arsenic to his nightly shandygaff. She likes the Kindly Old Country Doctor, and asks him to join her soothing ritual. He says something to the effect of "I should be glad of some tea. But don't send for another cup. I'll have mine in this basin, for I'm in rather a hurry."

Basin? Slop bowl? Shallow saucer? Surely a genteel accused murderess on a country lawn in the twenties would not have been drinking from a "dish"!

Resentment of my self-invited indenture lessened as I grew up and out, and I made tea almost every afternoon for fellow-students in France, because I was a married woman and therefore could invite people to my room when they could not, and also because I had a gas ring, and even running water. And none of us had enough money to go more than once a month or so to Duthu or Michelin, the best tearooms in Dijon, where we could eat delicious pastries and ices instead of slabs of the cheapest local gingerbread called *pavé de santé*. When Mother came to Dijon in about 1930 and saw my prized tea equipment, she immediately bought me four pretty teacups and what she called "a decent pot." I still use it—an ugly Burgundian ceramic thing but with a good spout. ("It pours well.")

But after that, in my thirties, and then probably until death, my bitterness about the ceremony of Afternoon Tea, as seen by the pawn who makes and serves and then unserves it, has grown. By now, I can barely face it when even my dearest friends will "be along about teatime." I feel what is more irritation than boredom. Often I say, "Or a glass of wine?" But when they mean tea, for cultural or any other of a dozen reasons, good tea is what I give them, and I do it conscientiously and well, and feel about fourteen.

Grandmother taught me that tea must be hot and fresh, and of fine quality. Mother went on to show me that it tastes best served from pleasant and elegant utensils. I could never brew tea strong enough to trot a mouse on. Neither would I affect only porcelain, for tea served from a silver or even a pewter pot, if made properly, can be as good as that made in the rarest of chinaware. After all, water is usually boiled in metal before it is poured over the dried leaves, and then is stirred with a silver spoon, here in the Western world, so why quibble?

My grandmother died before tea bags became commonplace. I am thankful. My mother never admitted their existence. A friend has described them as boiled mice, and he is right, too, but I have some teas in little white bags for people who have never known anything else, and who are adept enough to leave the wee tail hanging over the edge of the cup. I am told that these mice are often dried out and used again.

I do not serve the black China tea that Grandmother liked for lunch. Occasionally, I serve black Russian tea, but mostly China greens, with beautiful names. I also serve herbal teas made of many leaves and blossoms (everything but alfalfa!), to people who are usually under thirty and prefer mugs to cups and saucers. I even have a silver teapot, although I prefer the good old mustard-and-green monster that Mother bought in Dijon, because it pours so truly. But I never do more than sniff the stuff, as its first steam rises. If I did, as I learned some forty years ago, I would probably fall on my face, or go whirling off in a skunk-drunk dance. In other words, tea is my poison.

In about 1942, I spent a night with two friends who were flat broke. I felt poor myself but did not realize that they actually had no money for toast for breakfast, much less butter or honey to put on it. I was worried for them, but we were young and strong, and we loved each other, as we still do. So we sat for about three hours drinking tea. There was nothing like sugar or milk or an old cookie to blanket it. We talked and laughed and came to great conclusions, and I should have remembered how Grandmother and Father and Mother grew pink-cheeked and chatty after a couple of cups of the lunchtime brew from Dublin. Instead, I finally drove off to meet my mother at Great-Aunt Maggie's and head back to Whittier, and almost at once I knew that I should not be behind the wheel.

I was a good driver, and had been since I was eleven and Father taught me—pure hell all the way, since, like most loving parents who must cope with pre-adolescent vacuities, he was harsh and mocking. Traffic laws were simple then, and there were often no white lines down the middle of roads and no red and green lights. I knew all the rules, including my father's firm dictum that I should always drive as if everybody else on the road were either drunk or crazy. And that day, full of good company and tea, I knew I was. Telephone poles were matchsticks, put there to be snapped off at a whim. Dogs trotting across the road were suddenly big trucks. Old ladies turned into moving vans. Everything was too bright, but very funny and made for my delight. And about half a mile from my long liquid breakfast I turned carefully down a side street and parked, and sat beaming happily through the tannic fog for about an hour, remembering how witty we all had been, how handsome and talented.

By the time I got to Great-Aunt Maggie's, Mother was plainly a little put out by my lateness, but I was sober. We drove home in a good mood, and although I never told her why I was tardy, that afternoon we sat pleasurably together by her fire over a cup of delicate green tea, and she did not see that I was not drinking it. But I did not drink tea then or ever again.

This deliberate and self-protective abstinence has often filled me with regret. I love the scent of good or fine tea freshly brewed. I like to serve it, in spite of my long resentment of the fuss/muss of tray and napkins and heated pot and water brought to boil, and then of tidying everything before the cook must stagger into the kitchen— long ago to get dinner on the table so that the Mister went to his meeting on time, and now so that I can ready things for less hurried dinings.

Was I warned so dangerously because of my anger at my own docility for all those years? Did I find myself high-drunk on fury and frustration, or on other chemicals, like caffeine? How can I know? For this maimed tea lover, one answer may be that the intoxication that lives in discovering the way our language can be used is headier than any herbal or fermented brew.

—M. F. K. Fisher

Part 1

A Very Brief Description of Tea Types

Throughout this book you'll be introduced to what may be new and exotic terminology for teas. Basically, all true teas (as opposed to herbal infusions) come from the same plant, *Camellia sinensis*. As more and more teas become available, particularly from China, we are discovering many relatives to this plant, varietals that are different in size and sometimes different in the numbers of leaves. Wild tea plants still flourish in parts of China, and one can only imagine that they are descendants of the plant that first fascinated the emperors and monks of history, and, of legend.

For our purposes, however, we will be concerned primarily with the classic two leaves and bud formation of the familiar *Camellia sinensis*. The larger of the two leaves is referred to as the pekoe leaf; sometimes orange pekoe, and is an anglicized variation of the Chinese word *pa-ko*, used to describe the down-like hairs found on the finest leaves. It is not, as some blenders would have you believe, a type of tea. There really is no such thing as an orange pekoe tea; it is usually a variety of teas blended to provide a pleasant and typically undistinctive brew and is habitually misnamed.

The bud we refer to is not a flower bud, but the bud of another leaf, and is the most prized, most sought after part of the tea plant for its exquisite delicacy in taste and appearance. Teas comprised of all buds are the most expensive and rather rare.

What makes teas so different in taste (and, therefore so fascinating) is how they are processed. To date, we have six basic categories: white, yellow and green teas; oolongs, blacks and Pu-ers. White and yellow teas are very rare, very delicate and, like green teas, barely processed. They are lightly steamed, sun-dried or pan-fried in very large woks and moved about in a circular motion by hand all around the wok to insure evenness in drying and uniformity in color. (And, yes, the hands of such craftsmen are toughened against the heat, yet still sensitive enough to know when to add or ease up on the pressure.)

Oolongs are fired for longer periods; these particular teas are very fragrant, and very distinct in their taste. The most prized of these are named for the Iron Goddess of Chinese legend, Ti Kwan Yin; hence, the most sought-after are also jet black in appearance, to look like iron.

Blacks are referred to as reds in China because even though they are black-ish in color, they brew up a distinctively reddish brew. These are the teas most westerners are familiar with, the ones most commonly imported from Sri Lanka (Ceylon) and India, although both countries have all types of teas. Your Earl Grey or English Breakfast will most frequently contain two or three black teas from Keemun (China), Assam (India) and/or Ceylon (Sri Lanka).

Pu-Ers are decidedly a China tea, aged, with a distinctive musty smell that reflects the bacteria found in it. Often referred to as Chinese penicillin, it is beneficial as a digestive, and healthful, especially as a grease cutter. It can be reddish in color but is most often brown to black and brews up a dark rich liquor.

Tea plucking is an arduous job, still done by hand, by laborers who work all day to pick a bushelful at most. These leaves are then dried and processed and may result in barely a pound of tea, so you can imagine how many people have to work so many days to provide you with your cup of tea.

Orthodox manufacture in India and Ceylon is a labor-intensive process, involving hand-rolling and hand-twisting of teas to uniform appearance. Similar hand-work in China results in teas that are uniform in color, shape and size. These processes are critical to providing a beautiful appearance in both the dried and the infused leaf, and the best tasting teas. Brokers and blenders are making concerted efforts to encourage the individual farmer or plantation owner to continue this hand-work rather than resorting to machinery.

Broken or cut leaves provide wonderful cups of teas, particularly if the CTC (Cut, Tear and Curl) processing is deliberate and careful. Designations following some tea names are your indicators: e.g. F.O.P. or B.O.P., (Flowery Orange Pekoe or Broken Orange Pekoe respectively). T is used to designate tip or tippy (see glossary); the golden or silvery tips of the edges of dried tea leaves indicating generally more fragrant and more flavorful teas of their particular category.

Like most people who are devotees, we urge you to explore many types of teas. The road to the ultimate cup of tea is a wonderful one, full of enchanting detours and delightful stopovers, and always fascinating. Enjoy!

The Teas of China

꒰ ꒱

The dizziness of too much possibility arises at the very thought of buying China tea. Yet, at present, the best quality and the most interesting examples are available from a very few American purveyors. The transformation of China from a mainly agricultural Marxist society into a modern market economy has been one of the most dramatic events of recent times. As recently as twenty-five years ago, all the tea in China was still cultivated and produced by hand. These time-honored techniques have mostly been duplicated by modern technology, so that over 70 percent of China's tea is now manufactured by machinery, including some of her most delicate types.

The former national tea monopoly remains in business only thanks to the national permit system which prevents individuals or factories from exporting on their own. Much of China's finest tea continues to be produced by traditional methods, and a growing number of rare and even legendary teas are now beginning to become available outside China. As her market economy gains ground, more and more farmers and factories withhold their best teas from the national monopoly to sell them for better prices to private companies. On the other hand, as more and more Chinese become able to afford teas of this quality, less and less will be available for export.

China is to tea what France is to wine, with Italy thrown in for good measure. Yunnan alone produces well over one hundred types of tea, and there are eighteen other tea-producing provinces. Piercing China's secrets has never been easy, and in our

time the dragon guarding all the tea in China has been a bureaucracy designed for Mao Tse-tung by Franz Kafka known as the China National Native Produce and Animal By-Product Import and Export Corporation. The idea of a nationwide monopoly on tea was tried by a Tang emperor as early as 785; a more recent precedent comes from the Imperial Horse and Tea Commission, which was responsible for mass-producing and marketing tea to non-Chinese until it was abolished in 1423, so corrupt had it become after five centuries of operation. (In its peak year, 1389, it bartered about a million pounds of tea with nomads beyond the Wall for some twenty thousand horses.) Its successor, in some respects at least, was the Imperial Tea Bureau, which, under the Qing (Manchu) dynasty, employed thousands of eunuchs (who would not be distracted from work by their libidos) to classify the vast amounts of tea produced throughout the Middle Kingdom. Over time, the classification system began to resemble a vast Chinese puzzle as the labeling of teas became more and more complicated. Amazingly, after the dynasty's collapse the Imperial Tea Bureau rumbled along under its own momentum, adding another hundred or so new tea names before its eventual dissolution in the 1920s.

The first Westerners to buy tea were soon elaborating a classification vocabulary of their own: "Pekoe" from *pak-ho*, "white hairs," referring to the down on unopened leaf bud or tip. "Souchong," from *siau-chung*, means "subvariety" in Fujian dialect, probably in reference to oolong. "Congou" for "black tea," derived from *kung-fu* (or *gongfu*), "skill and patience"; "Bohea" from *Wu-I*, the tea-growing mountains in Fujian. The Chinese called spring-flush (or plucking) green teas "before-the-rains" or *yu-tsien* tea. To eighteenth-century English ears *yu-tsien* sounded like "Hyson," the name of an East Indian Company director and tea merchant, and certain China green teas are sold as Hyson or Young Hyson to this day.

"Ten thousand," the Chinese say, when they mean a large number which nobody can specify exactly. "The ten thousand teas" would be their way of saying "all the tea in China," and that "guesstimate" sounds about right. The Communist attempt to deal with this age-old profusion took the form of establishing numbered quality standards for each tea sold. The highest commercial standard for Jasmine, for example, is 9101, followed by 9102, etc. The quality of each of these different standards vary but little from one year to the next, even though the quality of the harvests may be uneven. Each provincial branch of the tea monopoly blends the produce of its province to match the unvarying standards for each type of tea. They have become so scrupulously successful at this that China teas alone in the world are bought without the foreign importers' needing to sample them first. Each number corresponds to a well-defined degree of quality, just as mass market tea blends do in the West. This avoidance of estate names is justified by long practice.

"Tea, in China, is grown in small patches on the hillsides," wrote W. H. Ukers in 1935, "mostly by peasant proprietors, as one of several crops. Large estates . . . are unknown. The leaves are stripped from the bushes by the farmer and are partly manufactured. In this state they are sold to collectors, who resell them to tea *hongs* or factories, and the *hongs* in turn resell to middlemen who supply the foreign exporter." Although large estates and factories have undoubtedly existed since the days of the Tea and Horse Commission, much over half of China's tea was always a homegrown, handmade product of nameless peasant farmers.

Tea is not simply a product, it is also a practice, one which the Chinese have spent thousands of years bringing to perfection. Fine oolong shows its full force and breeding in the traditional kung-fu preparation, and the traditional covered cup, or *guywan*, provides the simplest, most satisfying way of enjoying green tea, among others. Every type of tea that's ever been invented is still made somewhere in China, the homeland of tea, which offers a wealth of pleasures available nowhere else on the planet.

C H I N A   G R E E N   T E A

*I*mperial China's last ambassador to the Court of St. James, the noble Prince Chung-Sze, once ordered a "tea-colored" Rolls-Royce to be shipped home to Shanghai. When the car arrived, His Excellency was distressed to find it the copper-penny color of Darjeeling instead of the gold-green color of China green tea he had in mind. "Tea" typically refers to green tea to the Chinese.

Green tea makes up more than half of China's tea crop, without even counting all the green made into scented tea. It is produced in every tea-growing district and province, and *ordinaire* may be exported as China Green Tea or by province name as Fujian, Guanxi, Hunan, etc., Green Tea.

Zucha ("Pearl Tea" or Gunpowder)

Gunpowder is what some eighteenth-century Englishman thought this tea looked like, though whether on account of its grayish-green color or its granular shape I cannot say. To the Chinese it's Zucha—"Pearl tea"—since each leaf is rolled into a tiny, compact ball. For this reason it also keeps best of any tea, green or black. The strong dark-green brew is not unpleasantly bitter. Since it is heavier than other teas, about half the usual amount of dry leaf is sufficient.

Gunpowder is probably the most popular green tea in the Muslim world and is drunk from Central Asia to Morocco, where it's the base for the locally beloved mint tea, for instance. It originated around Pingshui in northern Zheijiang and is now produced in neighboring Anhui and Jiangxi provinces as well. There's a noticeable variation between grades. The highest standard is packaged and marketed as "Temple of Heaven Special Grade."

Longjing or Lung Ching ("Dragon Well")

Longjing is the most renowned green tea in China and, probably, the world. It is of ancient origin, already known as Fragrant Forest White Cloud under the Tang dynasty, and in the tenth century it was likened to a beautiful woman in a famous poem by the Song Court official Su Dongpo. It comes from the hills overlooking Xihu or West Lake, just outside the beautiful old Song capital city of Hangzhou, and takes its modern name—already centuries old—from a well inhabited by a dragon, according to local lore. Not far away is Tiger Run Spring, long since considered the ideal water for brewing the tea that grows round about in this most ancient of Dragon Well gardens. It was here at

Wugong Temple on Shih Feng Shan or Lion Peak Mountain that the Manchu emperor Qianlong waited early one spring in the 1720s to drink tea freshly made from the year's first tea leaves. Eighteen of the oldest plants on the site were reserved by the emperor to provide Tribute Tea exclusively for his own pleasure. At the same season, in a guest house nearby, Mao Tse-tung drank the same tea with President Richard Nixon at their historic first meeting.

Perhaps the best thing to be said for Longjing is that it lives up to its legends. The Chinese praise it for "four uniques": jade color, vegetative aroma, mellow chestnut flavor and singular shape. Longjing looks remarkably flat and smooth and is slick to the touch. When the leaf is infused and opened, you can see that it consists largely of intact buds. Its light emerald liquor has an intriguing and delicious aroma and taste, like fresh-mown hay with a haunting, distant sweetness. It is a tea to write poetry by. Each pound consists of thirty to forty thousand hand-plucked shoots which are allowed eight to ten hours for evaporation and then scooped into a hot wok and manipulated by hand for up to fifteen minutes. The tea maker's hands never rest or leave the wok during this period, and unless temperature, hand pressure and timing are perfect, the quality suffers irremediable harm. After an hour's cooling off, the tea is returned to the wok for a shorter period at a lower heat just prior to sifting and packing. The growing district includes numerous villages where the entire population is involved in tea production.

Flush can be picked up to thirty times from April through October, but the best is always harvested "before the rains," traditionally before the Ching Ming festival on April 5. I have never tasted a Dragon Well I didn't enjoy, and I cannot name another green tea capable of such refinement.

There's a real danger of becoming something of a Dragon Well snob once you've been carried to such heights. China Tea, Inc., the national monopoly, exports seven grades: Superior, Special and grades 1 down to 5. (All are shipped hermetically sealed in a nitrogen atmosphere for maximum freshness. Most U.S.-sold Dragon Well is third or fourth grade. If the leaf has a yellowish tinge, the tea is already growing stale.) All of these grades are enjoyable enough. Sometimes found in Chinatown shops is a packaged-in-China "Superfine" grade. The problem with buying packaged tea is you never know if it's fresh, but when it is, it begins to show just how excellent this tea can be. Most Americans can hope to go no further.

To see just how extraordinary Dragon Well can be, you have to obtain it from somebody who has just returned from a springtime pilgrimage to Hangzhou. David Hoffman of Silk Road Teas has brought back small amounts, and some years the Mark T. Wendell Company obtains a fine example. Indubitably the best entering the country, however, is always that procured by Roy Fong of Imperial Tea Court. The finest grade he obtains is called Queshe or Sparrow's Tongue, the smallest possible leaf bud with one intensely green baby leaf. It was for tea of this quality that the old emperors visited the Dragon Well gardens in spring. Its noticeably paler liquor is both more delicate and more intensely sweet, not to mention more unbelievably aromatic, than any other Dragon Well. Mr. Fong is able to supervise plucking and production each year. The result is tea from heaven—a voluptuous, Chinese heaven rarely entered by foreigners. One taste and one is confident of remembering this tea perfectly in the life to come.

BiLuoChun or Pi Lo Chun ("Green Snail Spring")

A close neighbor of Longjing, BiLuoChun comes from Jiangsu province just inland from Shanghai. For centuries this tea was called Astounding Fragrance until given its present name by the great Manchu emperor Kang-Xi around 1700 when he toured the tea district one spring. (He also stopped at the Longjing gardens.) The name translates as "Green Snail (or Conch) Spring" and refers possibly to the tightly rolled spirals of the finished leaf or to the way the leaf spirals downward through the water when infusing. Legend claimed the tea's "astounding fragrance" derives from the peach, plum and apricot trees planted between the rows of bushes, since the trees would be in full blossom when the earliest tea leaves unfold, but of course, they do not actually absorb foreign scents. Only a bud and a half-unfurled single leaf from the earliest springtime harvest go into BiLuoChun; it takes some sixty to seventy thousand of these leaf-bud sets to make a single pound of dry leaf. In a unique procedure, this very fluffy and downy-looking tea is manufactured entirely by hand and is still fired over wood—not electric—heat.

Tea is a great teacher of geography. When sipping this famous elixir, try to picture a mountain with twin peaks rising beside a lake called Taihu. This lake is located where Zhejiang and Anhui meet Jiangsu, not far inland from Shanghai. Yixing, the ancient pottery center, is located on its shores opposite the region where the greatest BiLuoChun is grown.

Brewing BiLuoChun requires skill because of its extreme delicacy. The water temperature should be as low as possible and still obtain an infusion, that is, well under the 180 degrees Farenheit which is ideal for Dragon Well. (And the cooler the water, the longer the time required for steeping, as a rule.) No water is poured on the leaf, but rather, it is the leaf that is added to the water in the cup. The Chinese like to observe the "agony of the leaves," their dancing and unfurling, and, in cases of wonderfully animated leaf like BiLuoChun, glasses are used. Part of the tea's charm is to observe the corkscrew spiral of each leaf sinking from surface to bottom. Of course, it can also be enjoyed looking down into a *guywan.* The two government-marketed grades of "Pi Lo Chun," as it is still labeled, give only the faintest notion of the glory of this tea. As with Longjing, the best advice is to buy the most expensive you can possibly afford from a trusted source.

Huangshan Mao Feng and Company: China's Ten Most Famous Teas

With their love of lists and categories, the Chinese have settled on their "Ten Most Famous Teas." The list includes Longjing and BiLuoChun along with four other greens, one white, two oolongs and a single black tea. The most famous greens include legendary Huangshan Mao Feng from Anjui province, where it is grown around Huangshan, one of China's most celebrated mountains. Another from Anhui is Liuan Guapian, or "Melon Slice," as greatly beloved throughout China as it is unknown outside. These teas were first introduced to the U.S. market by Imperial Tea Court. Any lover of green teas who makes their acquaintance will soon find it hard to imagine life without them.

The other "most famous" green teas are apparently hard to find even inside China. They are Xinyang Maojian from Henan province, on the edge of the arid northern plain, and Dujun Maojian from Guizhou. The white tea among the ten is Junshan Yinzhen. Anxi Ti Kuan Yin and Wu-I Yencha are the oolongs and Keemun the solitary black tea included.

Other China Green Teas

MEECHA ("EYEBROW") TEAS

This is chiefly worth mentioning because the Meecha category usually includes more actual tonnage of green tea than any other kind made in China—it is the national *ordinaire*. The processed leaf resembles an eyebrow and thus received its name. Chunmee, or "Precious Eyebrow," refers to a lady's plucked and finely formed brows, suggested by the delicate curve of the leaf. Chunmee is the chief green type exported, usually as "Hyson" or "Young Hyson."

"Anhui green tea was first processed in the seventeenth century. It is the earliest ancestor of Meecha," avers the catalog of the Anhui Province Branch of China Tea, Inc., the national monopoly. This became the most common form of loose-leaf tea, which evolved slowly but finally swept China under the Ming to become the drink of the Chinese masses both within and beyond the tea-producing regions of the country. Though most are unexceptional, Special Chunmee has a distinct plumlike flavor and an egg yolk yellow color.

YUNWU ("CLOUD AND MIST") TEAS

The tea plant often thrives best on cloud-and-mist-covered elevations. Besides being a source of water and keeping the leaves moist as they grow, the cloud seas surrounding certain mountains at certain times of the year also screen the plants from direct sunlight. As a result, the leaf develops more slowly and also compensates chemically for the absence of sun. The amount of chlorophyll in the leaf is increased, and less caffeine develops. This altered chemistry produces quite an unusual flavor, which is brought out by a variety of special procedures developed over the centuries for the manufacture of the different Yunwu teas, a category as tiny in total volume produced as Chunmee is huge. As ancient as the hermit tradition which gave birth to them, all of these teas are as legendary and *sui generis* as Huiming, for instance, a tea made at a Taoist monastery on a sacred mountain. Tienmu Qingding, Tientai and Lushan Yunwu are other famous names to conjure with.

MAOJIAN ("HAIR POINT") TEAS

"Hair Point" refers to the unopened leaf bud covered with fine downy hairs. When these are plucked, usually together with a single leaf, in the first days of the spring flush, the small quantity of tea that results is often called a Maojian tea, as in Guzhang Maojian, Weishan Maojian, Xinyang Maojian, Jiukeng Maojian and others, including the most famous of them all, Dujun Maojian (formerly known as Kweichow or Douyun Maojian). When infused, Dujun's silvery leaf rises and falls rhythmically in the water—a good reason for making it in glasses to watch—and finally comes to rest standing upright like a miniature forest of *dujun*, or "flagged spears." These are also legendary teas. They must be drunk fresh and are only slightly less difficult to acquire than the Yunwu.

ESHAN PEKOE AND OTHERS

Superb and from Yunnan, Eshan is an example of the wonders awaiting discovery once the intrepid taster finds a source for authentic China teas. Opposite the BiLuo-Chun district on the southern shore of Lake Taihu lies Guzhu, where an ancient Tang dynasty Tribute Tea called Guzhu Zisun, or "Purple Bamboo Shoot" is still grown. This tea, named for its bamboolike pointed tips, is prized for its sweet aftertaste.

CHINA   WHITE   TEA

Yinzhen ("Silver Needles")

White tea is the veal of tea and represents one of the pinnacles of refinement in tea's long history, and was singled out by the Emperor Huizong (who ruled from 1101 to 1125) as the rarest and finest tea produced in all his realm. Very much in this tradition is Junshan Yinzhen, the white tea from Hunan currently reckoned among China's Ten Most Famous. (It was also famous in the Tang dynasty over a thousand years ago.) It is packaged and sold in 1.5-gram individual servings for three dollars each, making it perhaps the costliest tea in the world. Junshan is the name of the mountain where it originates, and "Yinzhen" translates as "Silver Needles," the general name for white tea of this sort. Plucked in the forty-eight hours or less between the time the first buds become fully mature and the time they open, these are "flowery pekoe" leaves, technically speaking, and give the ultimate delicacy in flavor.

Most Yinzhen today comes from Fujian, plus some from Guangxi. Steaming is part of its preparation; rolling and firing are not. It should be prepared a cup at a time. There is always danger of using too little leaf, because it looks so much larger than it weighs. Otherwise, it's hard to go wrong in preparing this tea, though the water should never be boiling. There's no caffeine and no tannin, just the freshest flavor with an evanescent sweetness in the aftertaste which lingers on and on. The Chinese sometimes add a dried rosebud or chrysanthemum flower to enhance this perfection.

Shou Mei ("Longevity Brow")

This Chinese name may be variously spelled—Shou Mei is also Shoumee, Sowmee or (my favorite) Show Mee. It means "Longevity Eyebrow" and refers to the bushy brows of an old man, which the raggedy leaf is supposed to suggest. Made from lightly steamed and unrolled, sun-dried leaf, it is rarely expensive and very popular with Cantonese and overseas Chinese. The best leaf has a faintly peppery quality to the flavor. Superior Shou Mei is distinguishable from the rest by younger, silver-edged leaf of delicate beauty and more flowery taste.

Bai Mudan or Pai Mu Tan ("White Peony")

Mudan, usually about one inch round, are created by tying together many leaves to form the shape of a flower. When infused it "blossoms" from the weight of the water to form a "peony". Mudan are also made from red teas.

CHINA OOLONG TEA

Black (fully fermented) and oolong (semifermented) teas are a fairly recent development, if anything may be called recent in China, originating only a century or so before Columbus. Fermentation is what distinguishes these types from green tea, although nothing really "ferments" or produces alcohol. "Fermentation" is like "tannin" (see glossary), another tea term inherited from previous centuries' faulty understanding of chemistry. While our chemical misunderstanding has been corrected, our vocabulary has not. The polyphenols found in tea are totally unrelated to the tannic acid in oak bark which tans leather, but "tannins" they continue to be called, just as "fermentation" has still not given way to the more accurate term, "oxidation." And this is what makes oolong and black teas. "Oolong," by the way, is an anglicization of *Wu Lung*, or "Black Dragon."

Fresh leaf is juicy and brittle enough to snap if bent. If allowed to wither in sunlight or hot air, however, much of its 70 percent moisture content evaporates, and the leaf becomes flaccid enough to bend without breaking. When making green tea, the leaf is then dried and rolled at the same time, traditionally in hot woks. Rolling gives the tea leaf its shape; the tightness of the lengthwise roll is called the "twist." The tighter the twist, the more time and skill the tea maker employed in the rolling, generally speaking. To make green tea, withered leaf is basically put into a wok and rolled over diminishing heat until the leaves rustle like paper and it's done. Different rolling techniques produce different twists, or leaf styles—Chunmee, Gunpowder, you name it.

For black or oolong tea, leaf is rolled without heat after withering. Once this green and sticky mass is bruised and broken open so that its juices are exposed to the air, it is then spread out to oxidize and, like a freshly sliced apple, it quickly starts to turn brown. Along with a change in color, this exposure to the air produces fragrance. If allowed to "ferment" completely, the leaf turns its darkest and when fired becomes black tea.

Oolong tea is not fully fermented, though the meaning of "semifermented" varies from about 60 percent for classic Formosa oolongs to as little as 14 percent for some "green" oolongs made on the Mainland. (On Taiwan the latter would be termed a *pouchong* tea. Technically speaking, most of its polyphenol content remains unoxidized.) About thirty chemicals called polyphenols make up the wrongly named "tannins" which account for flavor in tea. Polyphenols are completely unoxidized in unfermented green tea, of course, and the color of the liquor is a pale green derived from chlorophyll and plant pigments alone. It is the oxidized polyphenols, together with oxidized essential oils, which give oolong and black teas reddish color, luscious body, sweet fragrance and deep flavor.

Obviously, the key to obtaining the desired results is to stop the fermentation process at just the right moment. The Chinese learned to accomplish this by throwing the leaf into very hot woks to steam and crackle. It is stirred very fast to keep it from scorching or sticking. Periodically it is taken out to be cooled and rolled some more, then thrown back into progressively cooler woks for further firing, finally to be rendered crisp and dry in baskets over low charcoal fires. The Chinese call fire "the teacher of tea." Except that electric power has replaced charcoal heat, this procedure is unchanged in the manufacture of any first-rate China Oolong.

Oolong is produced chiefly in Fujian province, although notable examples are made in Guangdong and elsewhere. The best generally comes from leaf plucked in June, and not early spring, because it must be made from a single mature leaf—not two young leaves and a bud. Two subvarieties of the tea plant have been found ideal for producing oolong—Shuixian and Ti Kuan Yin—but a multitude of other names are also worth remembering: Fenghuang Dancong, for instance, which is made from straight-trunk tea trees in Guangdong which grow so tall that ladders must be used to pluck the leaf. The typical Chinese restaurant-grade oolong provides no hint of what this tea can be, or how widely examples can differ.

Wu-I Yencha ("Bohea Rock Tea")

Bohea is the anglicized version of *Wu-I*, the name of the famous tea-growing mountains of Fujian province which are said to look like "how Disneyland would do China." Most Bohea was probably oolong, transported on a forty-day journey along the winding and toilsome "tea highway" to Canton by coolie, two chests to a man, without a single chest allowed to ever touch the ground. The nearby port of Fuzhou, opposite Taiwan, was not opened to European trade until 1833, following the Opium Wars. But it's a safe bet that neither then nor now has any of the most famous Bohea been shipped abroad. It's about as rare as Chateau d'Yquem, and about as costly.

The legendary oolong that is known—though rarely sampled—throughout China comes from an area of about eight square miles traversed by the Min River far from its mouth at Fuzhou. Small clumps of tea bushes grow along the stream higgledy-piggledy among boulders and cabbages, some of it all but inaccessible high up on cliffs, some in larger patches. A few of these bushes are over a thousand years old. All bushes were planted in identical soils but attempts to reproduce them have failed even when clones of ancient bushes were planted. Cultivation, pruning and production rests in the hands of only seventy families in all. The production is minuscule and the teas are named after the particular cliff or peak where the bushes grow, fanciful Chinese names like Hairy Crab, Buddha Hand, Black Heap, Red Border, and Clear Fragrance. Most famous of all, probably, is Great Scarlet Robe, or Da Hong Pao, as it has been known since Ming times at least. Most Wu-I oolong is decidedly *not* Yencha (the unreachable ancient bushes) and most is probably machine-made today, but it's almost always enjoyable and superior to generic oolongs.

Shuixian ("Water Sprite" or "Narcissus")

This particular subvariety of tea plant has a single trunk and few branches with unusually thick, glossy leaves that require special processing. I've rarely tasted any Shuixian to compare with the better Ti Kuan Yin oolongs.

Ti Kuan Yin ("Iron Kuan Yin")

Oolong teas are prized for their sweet fragrance and their luxurious, silky taste, an achievement resulting from its partial "fermentation" or drying process. They are indeed the epitome of elegance in teas. Most prized among the China oolongs is a type named for a goddess of Chinese legend, Kuan Yin. Always depicted as a willowy figure, with a beautiful face, exquisite hands and a demeanor of utmost gentleness and kindness, she is sometimes known as the Goddess of Mercy and sometimes likened to the Bodhisattva Kuan Yin of Buddhism or the Madonna of Christianity who make various appearances and often work miracles.

The tea named Ti Kuan Yin is based on a legend that recalls how Kuan Yin appeared one night to a devotee named Wei, a simple farmer in Shaxian ("Sand") County, who dedicated himself to maintaining a dilapidated local temple that housed a statue of the goddess which was made of iron (Ti in Chinese). Kuan Yin directed him to a treasure which she told him would endure for generations, provided he shared it with his neighbors. When he observed the treasure, all Wei found was a humble tea sprout, yet he obeyed the goddess, caring for it meticulously. After only two years, a very short time for a tea plant to mature, this modest sprout yielded a pound of finished leaf as its first crop that was unlike any other tea Wei had ever tasted. Its brew was unusually fragrant, and it stood up to one infusion after another. In time Wei was able to give cuttings of this wonderful plant to all his neighbors, and to this day Wu-I farmers continue to benefit from this gift from the Iron Goddess, Ti Kuan Yin.

Any Ti Kuan Yin produces superior oolong, and Ti Kuan Yin from Fujian's Anxi County, near the coast, is one of China's Ten Most Famous Teas. Not content to leave it at that, the Chinese traditionally designate that the very best comes from the Anxi Province: "Monkey-Picked" Ti Kuan Yin. The idea goes back to Wu-I Yencha, those unreachable ancient bushes growing high up on cliffs where monkeys live, but Chinese folklore has embellished this notion beyond any single explanation. Suffice it that any "Monkey-Picked" oolong is one the merchant takes enormous pride in; more you may believe at your own risk.

In south China, Ti Kuan Yin is often prepared kung-fu style and drunk from thimble cups. Made this way, it ranks with the strongest teas anywhere, yet retains its great delicacy. For intensity of aroma, fruitiness and depth of flavor it has no equal anywhere, in any preparation.

CHINA BLACK TEA

Few Chinese prize any sort of black tea, no matter how good. The workers who produce Keemun itself drink green tea. Black tea was originally made exclusively for export to barbarians, and one judges that this continues to be the case. Through an irony of history, some of China's leading black tea customers—the Manchu—happened to take over the Celestial Kingdom in 1644, and suddenly black tea production received encouragement from the throne itself. On the other hand, the authoritative W. H. Ukers claims Americans began to buy black tea only in 1828. At that time it was known as "Congou," a corruption of "kung-fu" (*gongfu*), meaning "expenditure of time and effort," probably in reference to the extra steps involved in black tea manufacture. Congou is still the international trade name for China blacks, but the Chinese call it *hongcha*, or "red tea."

Qimen ("Keemun")

Keemun is the grand seigneur of all China's black teas and one of the three or four best black teas in the world. The flavor almost sings—a matchless taste and aroma that reminds one of toast hot from the oven. (I think it smells like a dying rose.) Because of this unsurpassed depth and richness of flavor, Keemun takes extremely well to milk and even sugar.

It is erroneously thought to be the "original" English breakfast tea, though actually the English had been drinking black tea with breakfast long before Keemun was first produced in 1875. Qimen County, from which the name comes, is in Anhui province and had produced only green tea until then. Yu Qianchen, a young mandarin who had been unjustly disgraced and dismissed from the civil service, had learned in Fujian how to make the black Congou tea that was then in demand for export to England. Back home, he persuaded his father to establish factories in three villages, and Keemun was born.

Keemun is made from a particular subvariety of tea plant which, according to Chinese sources, is "full of the flavor of myrcenal, the chief constituent of the high flavor of Keemun Congou." Myrcenal, if you look it up, turns out to be an essential oil occurring in bay leaves and elsewhere but not, interestingly, in any other tea plant. It imparts an underlying sweetness as of ripe fruit to this very subtle tea, which has brilliant reddish-orange liquor and relatively little astringency. The famous rich aroma is highly distinctive and penetrating without being floral or perfumey. Keemun lovers often add a pinch of Darjeeling to the pot to make the flavor fairly shine.

Coming from hilly country some two to three thousand feet above sea level, Keemun is not a high-grown tea. There are four harvests, beginning with first flush in April and continuing through second, third and autumnal flushes. These are not sold separately, however, but are blended together in the five Standards, of which the best are 1110 and 1121. All Keemun is distinctive and much is superior. Then one discovers Hao Ya and Mao Feng, which are superb.

In a good year, a maximum of four hundred kilos of Hao Ya A and eight hundred of Hao Ya B are produced from the earliest spring flush. The leaf is tiny and black as asphalt after dark and tastes like Keemun in excelsis. These are teas for which reservations are required, and further praise unnecessary. Mao Feng is handmade mature leaf, long and curly, of a delicacy surpassing even Hao Ya, if such a thing be possible. The tea is light, its unique Keemun sweetness so surprisingly nuanced and many layered that one feels adding milk would be sacrilegious.

Yunnan

As trans-Himalayan crows fly, China's Yunnan ("South Cloud") province is not far from Assam in India. This region, bordering Tibet, Burma, Laos and Vietnam is thought to be the place where the tea plant originated. A wild specimen growing there is over one hundred feet tall and some 1,700 years old, making it one of the oldest plants on earth. Yunnan is also home to 260 out of the 320 subvarieties of tea known in China. Due to its remoteness and its high, impenetrable mountains, the assimilation of this highland region only began in the days of Kublai Khan and is incomplete even today. Although production of black tea did not begin in Yunnan until 1939, it now produces more black tea than any other province in China—and what tea it is!

No tea is easier to identify, or harder to miss, than Yunnan tea. It is made from the Dayeh ("Broad-Leafed") subvariety native to Yunnan, chiefly in the southernmost part of the province around Menghai. The leaf is so unbelievably tippy, or characterized by a light-colored point on the end, it is often khaki-colored, and the flavor has an unusual peppery quality. French tea man Jacques Jumeau-Lafond calls it "the mocha of tea," so rich, strong and straightforward is its character. The best Yunnan black tea of my experience is not made for export and sells in China for something like twenty-five dollars per quarter pound, while the worst I've ever tasted seemed pretty damned good.

Other China Congous

These are impossible to discount yet too numerous to mention, at least not in the same breath with Keemun or Yunnan. Ching Wo from Fujian is almost the only name to survive from the long, sad decline of China's old-time tea trade abroad. A hundred years ago people could call for I Chang, Ningchow, Pakling or Kintuck black teas and appreciate the differences among them. Panyong and Paklum types are still produced in south China. Sichuan produces noteworthy black teas, and Hubei makes a rather splendid one called Keemun Ji Hong. Curiosity seekers might note that Hainan black is best avoided, and Liupao from Guangxi is flavored with betel nut.

China Pu-Er Teas

This is a large and important category of teas virtually unknown outside China. The manufacture of Pu-Er tea is still ranked among China's state secrets, and outsiders are never allowed to see how it is made. This secrecy was well established by the Ming dynasty, when even trespassing in the tea gardens was a capital offense. Pu-Er is a market town in central Yunnan where this tea was traditionally gathered from round about for shipment to the rest of the country. It was already ancient when first discovered by the troops of Kublai Khan sent to annex Yunnan to his empire, and generations of Chinese commoners and connoisseurs have sworn by the stuff ever since. The U.S. Tea Examiner rejects any shipments of Pu-Er he comes across on account of its musty quality, which is disallowed by statutes. So far Chinese importers have gotten nowhere arguing that this particular kind of mustiness is induced at great effort and is exactly what the tea is supposed to have. Because of its well-attested medicinal qualities, however, Pu-Er tea continues to find its way into the country.

"Old," "elemental" and "earthy" might be the first words occurring to those unaccustomed to the flavor of Pu-Er. It is made chiefly from the Dayeh ("Broad-Leafed") tea variety responsible for Yunnan's great black tea. After fermentation the tea is inoculated with a kind of bacterium and allowed to undergo a secondary fermentation, so to speak, which develops its special character. The famous mustiness can be quite fierce in cheaper, younger examples, but the best is allowed to age and mellow. It can be stored for a half a century or longer. Prized antique teas sell for many hundreds of dollars per pound in Taiwan and Hong Kong. The Chinese drink it after greasy foods, and often on other occasions, both as a pleasure and as a health measure. Modern science has not investigated all the benefits claimed for Pu-Er, but its effectiveness in reducing cholesterol has been thoroughly established in tests at Hôpital St. Antoine in Paris and elsewhere. It is not the first time the ancient Chinese have been proven right.

Pu-Er can be an elegant, delicious tea—the liquor a deep blackish red and the mustiness hardly detectable. It has little caffeine, and the unique flavor is deep and rich, to be enjoyed with food or by itself. Whether prepared kung-fu style or by the individual cup, it yields multiple infusions. Most Pu-Er sold in Chinatowns is in compressed form, like the rather raw-tasting Toucha. Superior quality loose-leaf Pu-Er is almost impossible to find. Its healthful benefits as a digestif are legendary and it will soon be more readily available.

The Teas of India

❧ ❧

With over one million acres under tea, India is the world's largest tea producer and consumer, at least in the absence of reliable statistics for China. Most of this vast production (approaching 800 million kilos) is no doubt eminently forgettable *ordinaire*, but a high percentage of the world's finest black teas also come from India, and not always from the most famous districts. The economics of CTC (crush-tear-curl) machine production has inexorably driven down the amount of tea produced by the old-fashioned orthodox method—only 16 percent of the total in 1994, down from some 30 percent only five years earlier. With its granulated rather than whole or broken leaves, CTC tea requires less labor to produce and yields more cups to the pound. The best CTC teas are nothing to sniff at and occasionally are exceptionally flavorful. On the other hand, they never equal and far less surpass the finest Assam, Darjeeling or Nilgiri teas of orthodox manufacture. No CTC Darjeeling or Nilgiri is produced, to the best of my knowledge. Fair-quality green tea is also produced in India, notably in the Kangra and Mandi districts, but sometimes in Darjeeling (Risheehat) and Nilgiri.

ASSAM

The aroma of Assam tea is usually quite pungent and the flavor round and agreeably powerful. These sturdy, "generous" teas are unfailingly full-bodied but are best known

for a characteristic "malty" flavor. This quality is not always present, but is immediately recognizable and sets Assam apart from all other black teas. Unlike most of the better blacks, Assam is a low-grown tea. The dry leaf is often full of tawny-colored tips, a sign the youngest leaf—actually the unopened leaf bud—was used. The few uncommonly delicate and fruity Assams I've found were extremely tippy, sometimes to the point of looking like blond tobacco. Very occasionally an Assam is sold as "first flush." The most beautiful and most carefully manufactured is graded FTGFOP1, for Fancy Tippy Golden Flowery Orange Pekoe Number One. Unlike Darjeeling and other regions, Assam doesn't seem to suffer any generally poor seasons or years.

Even purists should try these teas with milk and sugar. Orange-red to dark red in color, Assam takes to milk perhaps better than any other black tea due to its unusually high tannin content. The addition of a little milk turns its dark liquor a bright red-brown, in contrast to the bright golden color that Ceylons turn. Milk gives Darjeeling a grayish cast.

DARJEELING

The better the Darjeeling, the harder it is to describe the taste. Its world-wide fame rests on its unique qualities, like Cuban cigars or French champagne. At its best, Darjeeling is a tea to wax ecstatic over, but unfortunately for the Darjeeling lover, it is rarely at its best. Like the quest for the perfect hamburger or a superlative California pinot noir, the search for the best Darjeeling is full of hopes and disappointments.

Over 110 million pounds of "Darjeeling" are sold each year, although the district produces only about 22 million pounds all told. One's best guarantee of obtaining the genuine article is either knowing your purveyor or recognizing the Indian-government-approved logo which was finally introduced in 1994 to protect the "Darjeeling" appellation. Single-estate tea from premium gardens like Castleton, Namring, Jungpana and others have long since become international status symbols, but these names alone cannot guarantee top quality teas. Their best teas are but a fraction of their total production—perhaps ten percent of Castleton's approximately thirty-five thousand kilos each year. The rest, though always costly, may often be outclassed by teas from virtually unknown gardens.

Darjeeling (altitude 6,500 feet) is a town in the foothills of the Himalayas within view of Kanchenjunga, the world's third highest peak. At one time there were some two hundred separate tea gardens, but these have been combined, renamed and consolidated under new owners until today Indian government figures indicate only seventy-two distinct gardens. A classification like Bordeaux's, now obsolete, once recognized twelve First-Class, twenty-two Second-Class and twenty-six Third-Class gardens ranging in elevation from under 2,000 to almost 7,000 feet and covering approximately nineteen thousand acres. Both quality and yield vary greatly at different altitudes; the higher grown the tea, the better it is in most cases.

Since rainfall and sunshine vary wildly throughout the district, there's no predicting which gardens will enjoy the most favorable conditions from season to season or from year to year. Disaster strikes an entire crop sometimes; even then, a few gardens may manage to make exceptional teas. Careful shopping will turn up a goodly number of these most years, and once or twice a decade the teas are simply spectacular: These are what the cult of Darjeeling lives for, in prayerful but impatient expectation.

Slopes of less than 45 degrees are considered almost level by Darjeeling standards; planting on slopes up to 60 or 70 degrees is the rule rather than the exception. Adding to the difficulty of harvest, most of the plants are China or China hybrid types (or *jats*) which are small leafed compared to the Assam plant. It takes some 15,000 shoots of two leaves and a bud to make up one kilogram of dry leaf, whereas only 7,500 shoots produce the same weight of finished tea made from the broad-leaf Assam *jat*.

There are three different crops or "flushes" each year, and the differences between these pickings are unmistakable, just as differences between gardens of the same teas may vary from one another. To generalize broadly:

First Flush: Darjeeling tea bushes begin waking up from winter dormancy following light rains in early March. First Flush is picked from then through early May. The crop is always small and the tea is one of the world's most expensive. Adverse weather sometimes renders the whole crop a disaster. Its unique quality comes from growing in bright sunshine but in the cold crystalline Himalayan air of early spring. First Flush is a puckery young tea, almost as light as any green, flamboyantly aromatic with a remarkable flowery taste; it has great freshness and finesse, its flavors almost evanescent. This tea loses its lively freshness and fades rather quickly as a rule and thus is said to have no keeping quality, just as young Beaujolais does not. Drunk a few months or (better!) weeks after harvest, it can be unforgettable. (Note: Darjeeling in unopened chests mellows somewhat but does not begin to fade for well over a year, sometimes two. Once the chest is broached, the tea remains at its best for only a few months.)

Second Flush: Plucked in May and June until the rains set in, this is Darjeeling's annual organ peal. It is the biggest harvest of the year, and whatever character the crop has is now fully developed. This is a medium-bodied tea, though more full-bodied than First Flush, with unmistakable breeding and delicacy, yet powerfully astringent. Usually very aromatic with the flavor of ripe fruits, it also should be a lush tea, and most examples are too thin to be ideal. At its best, it has undeniably the most complex harmony of flavor and body of any black tea in the world, with notes of ripe fruit usually described as muscatel, though one may be reminded of black currants and almonds as well. Whether fully developed or not, it is this peculiarly muscatel fruitiness and its everlasting aftertaste which characterize Darjeeling flavor and which it shares with no other tea. Second flush is over by July, when the rains come. As elsewhere, rainy season leaf is quick growing, abundant and of little or no distinction.

Autumnal Flush: Harvested after the monsoon in September and October as the air cools and sunshine returns, this is another superior plucking. Afterward the plants go back into hibernation for the dry, chilly winter.

NILGIRI

High-grown black teas from the Blue Mountains (Nilgiri in Tamil) in southern India are among the finest produced anywhere. These mountains look out over the Indian Ocean toward Africa and are home to hundreds of tea estates at elevations comparable with Darjeeling's. Not since before World War II have they enjoyed comparable prestige (or prices) abroad, however, so that production declined to *ordinaire*, which was long employed as neutral tea-bag filler in the West. Later it was mostly destined for the former U.S.S.R. and Eastern Europe. Certain estates have always produced outstanding Nilgiri nevertheless, but these were seldom seen or appreciated outside India. Now that the South India teas have lost their traditional markets and are being forced to compete with teas from other regions in the world at large, a renaissance in quality seems under way, and lovers of fine tea are beginning to accord them new respect.

Drinking Nilgiri is a bit like discovering, say, the wines of Australia. Wow! Who knew? Fine Nilgiri is always soft, untannic tea, like Ceylon, with which it shares some similarities in taste. It has a woodsy fragrance like no other, however, and is the most forgiving of black teas, perhaps impossible to oversteep. The seasonally dry months of December through March produce the best Nilgiri each year. Sometimes these are among the world's most fragrant teas, but they are prone to fading within the year. All Nilgiri is manufactured by the orthodox method, and the leaf is always stylishly well twisted. Broken and OP (Orange Pekoe) grade teas from great gardens like Craigmore, Havukal, Chamraj, Anaimudi, Tiger Hill, Dunsandale and Colacumby—to go no further—are often spectacularly good, and yet self-effacing as a saint, ideal for quiet afternoon companionship. Because multiple infusions can be squeezed from its leaf, Nilgiri is the favorite tea to use for *chai* throughout India. *Chai*, sipped all day long by millions of Indians, should really be known as a tea drink, as it is completely (yet deliciously) adulterated with spices, overboiled and overcooked, and mixed with milk. It is the utter opposite of pure unblended simple tea. It is a concoction yet rivetingly delicious when made well. It's surprising how splendid such a humble tea can sometimes be.

Mr. Devan Shah of India Tea Importers is encouraging production of India's first hand-rolled oolong at Chamraj and green teas elsewhere. The special clonally reproduced tea plants which have come into bearing on the government-owned estate, Tiger Hill, and at Colacumby have established new heights in taste and fragrance of their teas. Somewhere in the region is said to be a garden planted with only China bushes over a century ago, a promise of amazing flavor. Ooty, the tea region's county seat, was formerly the hill station for raj officialdom from Madras, just as Darjeeling, at comparable altitudes, was for Calcutta. Ooty and Conoor, nearby, are picture-postcard bits of England set amidst mountain mist and tea garden green.

INDIA'S OTHER TEAS

Sikkim and Nepal

Sikkim, a principality India annexed not long ago, is but a stone's throw from the neighboring Darjeeling district and home to a single tea garden, Temi. This estate was pioneered by an English planter and now belongs to the government; it produces a rather splendid tea with Darjeeling-like taste and comportment but with greater forcefulness. Not Indian but from just across the nearby border comes Golden Nepal, not great tea but certainly not bad. Like the legendary tea of the closed kingdom of Bhutan, known but by hearsay, these rarities should be grouped with Darjeeling.

Dooars

This small district lies to the west of Assam and to the southeast of Darjeeling, just where the mountains begin to rise up from the Ganges plain, making Dooars subject to the same seasonal monsoons as its neighbors. Like them, it produces first, second and autumnal flush teas. These are low-grown teas, like Assam. They are less powerful than Assam but, like it, are thick-liquoring and flavorful, with a taste sometimes reminiscent of Darjeeling. They are now chiefly used in blends, and the name is seldom heard outside of India. Likely as not, Dooars leaf may sometimes be trucked up the mountain to be manufactured as "Darjeeling," one is told. The Autumnal Flush is supposed to be the best. Good Hope is probably the most famous Dooars garden.

Terai

The Moghuls must have given this region its name, for *terai* is a Persian (Farsi) word meaning "damp" and designating a low, malarious belt at the base of the Himalayas. The Terai lies on the plains due south of Darjeeling and west of Dooars, from which it is divided by the Teesta River. The gardens consist largely of China plants, which produce a light, sweet tea. In Germany, where fine teas are most sought after, first-flush Terai from the Kamala garden sells for more than some Darjeelings. Ord is another respected estate. Are we missing something here?

Travancore

South of the Nilgiris and divided from them by a gap of sixteen miles rises another mountain chain called the High Ranges or Kanan Devon, known under the British raj as the Cardamom Hills. Here in Kerala state is the location of Highgrown, the largest tea estate in all South India, and many others. The teas are almost without exception CTC (cut-tear-curl), earthy tasting and rarely found outside of India.

The Teas of Other Lands

✦

CEYLON

When Sri Lanka reverted to its original Sinhalese name in 1972, it was decided to retain "Ceylon" to designate its most famous (and commercially important) export. It is almost as misleading to generalize about Ceylon tea as about Indian, although the differences among Assam, Darjeeling, and Nilgiri are more striking than those among various Ceylon teas. Ceylons are the favorite choice of those who find Darjeeling too refined and Assam too robust. These subtle teas are long on flavor and short on show, and the differences among them are subtle. It requires considerable familiarity to be able to tell one from another, but the differences among Ceylon teas are far from imaginary. Common to the best of them is an understated elegance which it is impossible not to love.

Dimbulla, Uva and Nuwara Eliya are the principal district names to look out for, all of them high-grown teas. There are other names also, chiefly Maturata, Ratnapura, Galle and Kandy, which seems the least distinguished of the lot. These latter are low- and medium-grown teas but, depending on the garden, can be surprisingly good. "Mid-country" tea grows between two and four thousand feet, but Ceylon's reputation rests on the 40 percent of her production from higher altitudes. When hit by drought or unseasonable weather, these teas show it in the cup. Although each district has its specific *goût de terroir*, districts are on the whole emphasized less than the names of estates known for their high quality.

That said, it must be admitted that among the finest Ceylons are blends of teas from several gardens, districts, or harvests, though almost always high grown. Nor are they always so all-fired delicate: Broken and small-leaf Ceylons make particularly strong and lively teas. Ceylons usually show much blacker leaf than Indian teas, and their liquor is significantly less astringent, i.e., "tannic." These are not teas that call attention to themselves. The differences among them are created by Sri Lanka's peculiar geography.

Virtually all Ceylon tea, low grown or high, comes from the south part of the island surrounding the central massif which forms Sri Lanka's backbone. Besides altitude, the two monsoons are the principal determinant of tea quality. When and wherever it's raining, the tea grows like crazy but loses its distinctive quality. The tricky part is that the central massif experiences both monsoons, but on opposite slopes. During June and July, when the southwest monsoon is beating against the western mountainside it is a common experience to enter Pattipola railway tunnel in mist and rain and, in a few seconds, to emerge into brilliant sunshine in Uva on the other side of the island divide.

Uva and Maturata are on the eastern slopes facing Malaysia, where the best tea is produced in the dry months from May till September. Rains come from October to January from the northeast monsoon, which moves on up to the east coast of India toward Calcutta. On the opposite western slope facing Africa are Dimbulla, Nuwara and, lower down, Ratnapura and Galle. Here the southeast monsoon brings rains from March into July on its way up India's west coast toward Bombay. These districts produce their best from January into March.

Dimbulla

Perhaps the most famous name in Ceylon tea, this district in the western highlands produces its best in February and March. Teas of this season are somewhat less flowery than early Darjeeling but very aromatic all the same, fuller of body yet light, without any thickness and with none of Darjeeling's astringent bite. Dimbulla produces a golden liquor and mellow, medium-strong flavors, with a lingering aftertaste. The handsome black leaf is sometimes Pekoe grade but more usually OP.

DIMBULLA GARDENS:

Pettigallia, "Lord of the Orange Pekoes"
Radella
Diyagama
Theresia
Nadoototem

Nuwara Eliya (pronounced New-RAL-ya)

Nuwara Eliya is indisputably among the world's greatest black teas. The district comprises some of the highest altitudes in Sri Lanka, with tea growing at six thousand to seven thousand feet. The OP is typically thin, long and wiry leaf, jet black, which calls for long steepings, up to seven or more minutes. It yields a medium-bodied, lightly astringent liquor. There is usually a haunting sweetness underlying the woody flavor of this soft tea, and a delicious aroma, sometimes of honeysuckle. For some reason this "champagne of Ceylon teas," justly so called, is seldom sold by garden name.

Uva

Tea plants grow more slowly and yield far less at higher altitudes, not to mention being harder to harvest. Uva and Nuwara teas come from gardens so steep, the newly plucked green leaf is often conveyed to the factory by aerial ropeways. While an experienced lowland plucker may gather up to sixty pounds of fresh leaf in a day, her upland sister is lucky to average half that. (Fine-plucking the flush—two leaves and a bud of tender fresh growth—is traditionally carried out by women everywhere tea is grown. There is no sign of machinery replacing this humble human labor.)

The September plucking is the best "seasonal" tea from this eastward-facing district—much stronger and more full-bodied than Dimbulla's best, and less complex perhaps, but more flavory and just as intensely aromatic. The Pekoe, OP and broken grades are all beautifully made. Golden-red liquors.

UVA GARDENS:

Dyraaba
Uva Highlands
Bombagalla
High Forest
Mlesna

FORMOSA (TAIWAN)

Formosa oolong is called Formosa instead of Taiwan for the same reason Ceylon is not called Sri Lanka. The Latin name the Portuguese gave the island, "formosa," aptly applies to its oolong tea. It translates as "shapely, beautiful," and Taiwan certainly produces some of the world's most beautiful oolong.

According to the Chinese, tea was never grown on Taiwan until 1850, when a certain Lin Fengchi first planted thirty-six shoots from Wu-I oolong plants which he had brought with him to Taiwan from Fujian, the great oolong-producing province on Mainland China which faces Taiwan. An Englishman named John Dodds introduced this tea to the world in 1869 when he dispatched a quarter million pounds of it to New York. A decade later the island was exporting ten million pounds every year. About twice that amount is exported annually today, mainly to Japan and the United States, while an equal amount is consumed domestically.

Taiwan's tea gardens, if that's the right word for patches cultivated by small farmers also raising other crops, are clustered in the northern end of the island, in Taipei and Xinzhu provinces, where seasons change and rains fall at intervals throughout the year. As in China, the tea is plucked from April through October, the quality diminishing from first to last. Oolong plucking requires taking three—not two—leaves and a bud. (Souchong is the name for that large third leaf which is plucked for making oolong.) Most of the seventy-two thousand acres under tea lie only a few hundred feet above sea level, another example of top-quality tea which is not high grown.

Although there are about 150 tea factories, a number of farmers produce the prized "handkerchief tea" themselves, so called from the small batches in which it's made and sold. There is also comparatively high grown Tung Ting Oolong, produced on the mountain of that name, which is the island's highest peak and its Holy Land of tea growing. The name "Tung Ting" (Dongding in Pinyin spelling) means "frozen summit," highly unlikely for its 2,300-foot elevation.

Oolong lies somewhere between green tea and black. The leaf is not killed with heat soon after plucking while it is still green, but it is not allowed to become completely withered and brown before firing either, which produces black tea. Oolong tea consists of leaf which has been allowed to wither and oxidize some, but not completely, before heat arrests further chemical change. This semifermented tea combines some qualities of both green and black tea but is in a class by itself.

The leaf is steamed prior to processing and then dried, in hot sunlight when possible, for about two hours. Several pounds at a time are then wrapped in a cotton blanket and carefully pressed by hand, so as not to tear the leaf. It is then allowed to wither in the shade for another two hours before the whole process (except steaming) is repeated three more times. Only then is the leaf rolled—without pressure and mostly by hand—for half an hour and pan-fired at about 250 degrees Fahrenheit until moisture content is reduced to no more than 10 percent. Grading by leaf size and addi-

tional basket firings at lower temperatures complete the manufacturing process. The dry leaf now has 3 percent moisture content and one-third less caffeine than black tea. It is said no tea on earth requires greater pains to produce.

The resulting tea is a crisp, open Souchong leaf, mostly reddish brown, but intermixed with green and black and liberally flecked with silver tips. Formosa oolong is traditionally about 60 percent fermented, in contrast to 12 to 40 percent for most Mainland China oolongs. (The closest Mainland tea in appearance is Shou Mei, a sun-dried white tea.) As with any large-leaf tea, you steep this one longer if made by the pot. Seven minutes seems just right—longer and you detract from its freshness somehow, shorter and you miss out on some flavor.

Fancy Oolong is extremely aromatic, a pale sparkling amber, and has none of black tea's bitterness or astringency—"no peaks, no bites" is how tea men describe it. Fancy Formosa oolong has the taste and aroma of ripe peaches; it is delicate yet lush, rich but light, and more deliciously fruity than any other tea. Apart from Tung Ting, these teas are not identified by garden or region but according to the grade assigned by the government Tea Inspection Office, and in this case the grade name actually denotes the quality of the tea. There are eight such grades altogether, but the names to remember are Fancy and Fanciest, though Extra Choice will do in a pinch.

JAPAN

Japan's tea industry rests on a multitude of small farmers with over 150,000 acres of tea under cultivation. They are so prodigiously efficient that yields are said to reach 1,500 pounds per acre, surely the world's record. Virtually all this tea is green and by far the greater part comes from Honshu, the main island, where the principal district is Shizuoka prefecture, about halfway between Tokyo and Kyoto. Japan's tea is among the most northerly grown in the world; there are three to four pluckings from May through mid-October, which total about 200 million pounds each year. Less than 1 percent of this total is exported, so that the only way to get to know Japanese tea well is to live there.

To judge by what is shipped abroad, Japanese tea is not graded by leaf size—both the finest and the poorest is a mixture of broken and unbroken leaf and includes dust. This is all pan-fired tea, a method used in China only for making Dragon Well and a very few other green teas. It seems fair to say the Japanese prize a grassy or sometimes fishy quality in their tea, in contrast to the earthy tastes favored by the Chinese. "Regrettably, the original Chinese plants taken to Japan have suffered from repeated cross-breeding. This has resulted in the inexplicable 'fishy' taste of most Japanese tea, which is vastly overpriced," comments scholar John C. Evans in *Tea in China*. Certain Japanese teas, in my experience, are most enjoyable if avoided altogether.

The most important names to recognize in Japanese tea seem to be these: Sencha, Gyokuro, Genmaicha and Bancha. In reverse order:

Bancha is a coarse tea made from both old and new leaf gathered in the last plucking of the year. Except in macrobiotic restaurants, it is seldom seen outside Japan but isn't bad, especially when the tea liquor is mixed with puffed rice or popcorn.

Genmaicha has a unique flavor obtained by mixing roasted barley, rice or popped corn with either Bancha or Sencha leaf Japanese teas.

Gyokuro, meaning "pearl dew," is one of the world's rarest and costliest teas. Darker green and slicker looking than other Japanese teas, it is made exclusively from the first pluckings of ancient Uji tea gardens near Kyoto. The bushes are covered with straw sunshades three weeks before they flush, which shields the new shoots from all direct sunlight and gives the tea its special character, and higher caffeine and lower tannin content. However obtained, Gyokuro certainly has an intensity of aroma and flavor rare for a green tea, a mouth-filling and complex flavor, more vegetative than herbaceous and surprising from such a pale-looking, greenish-gold liquor—a reminder that tea color is no guide to strength. The powdered tea employed in *chanoyu*, the Japanese tea ceremony, and known as Matcha, is said to be made from Gyokuro. Not all Gyokuro is created equal, moreover, and at its price—caveat emptor!

Sencha is sometimes labeled *ichiban-cha* (first flush) or *niban-cha* (second flush) and comprises some three-quarters of Japan's annual production. Quality varies from fair to finest. The characteristically long, flat dark-green leaves and fragments yield a pale greenish cup which tastes tannic and markedly grassy as a rule. As is typical of spring teas, *ichiban-cha* can be very delicate and fragrant.

Spiderleg is the generic name for a type of Sencha consisting of long, well-twisted leaves resembling pine needles or spider legs. It always tastes wonderfully nutty, quite different from other Sencha. **Ama-cha**—the name means "sweet tea" and should be taken literally—is traditionally served at Japanese temples on April 6, the annual festival of the Buddha's birth. The Chateau d'Yquem of teas, Ama-cha is an ideal dessert, with a marvellously minty and lingering aftertaste. Other Japanese teas I might list are known to me only by reputation.

JAVA, SUMATRA AND OTHER INDONESIAN COUNTRIES

In 1835 the frigate *Algiers* brought the first Java tea to Amsterdam. This was the first tea from anywhere outside China to reach Europe, a distinction universally but mistakenly accorded the first Assam tea shipped to London four years later. Holland's historic first has been overlooked because it did not lead to much until many years later. Tea growing got off to one false start after another in the Dutch East Indies, where it had been attempted sporadically since 1690. Java and Sumatra, the most important islands in this archipelago known today as Indonesia, had no successful tea plantations until the early years of this century after the introduction of Assam tea plants and mechanized manufacturing. Today, Indonesia has about 300,000 acres of tea and exports some 250 million pounds of black tea a year.

Java is home to fifty volcanoes, some well over six thousand feet high. Volcanic soils combined with this altitude and tropical rainfall should produce noteworthy teas, one might think, but alas, they are nowhere to be found. Holland's ex-colony continues to be her chief source of tea, and one supposes Dutch connoisseurs must have Java and Sumatra favorites which would compare with any Ceylon. If so, the secret is well guarded. Efforts to learn more from the Tea Board of Indonesia have elicited no reply.

Having thus damned and blasted the world's fourth-largest tea producer, I must confess that my curiosity is still aroused by European tea catalogs with entries like "Taloon, FOP: Great garden of Java. Best period harvest, beautiful golden-tipped whole leaves, aromatic taste, gentle bronze hint. A Five O'Clock tea." I think I'd like a hint of "gentle bronze." Regretfully, Indonesian teas all seem soft, untannic and quite plain to me so far. Goalpara is considered the premier growing region in Java. Sumatra's is Bah Butong.

KENYA

$\mathcal{O}$f all the countries which have turned to tea growing in the past century, Kenya is by far the most successful. The British introduced the crop in 1903. There are now some two million acres under cultivation, producing over 300 million pounds a year. For some years now the United States and Great Britain have imported more tea from Kenya than from Sri Lanka or India, though it is mainly used for mass-market blends. Kenya tea is but rarely sold unblended, although its popularity is increasing as its quality increases.

The Kenya Highlands, an extensive area on both sides of the Rift Valley between Mount Kenya and Lake Victoria, range in elevation from five to nine thousand feet and enjoy that second essential for growing good tea, copious rainfall. The soil, enriched over eons by volcanic ash, and the temperature, more moderate than Kenya's latitude might suggest, are ideal for tea, which can be harvested there year-round. All but a fraction of this is used for CTC (cut-tear-curl) production, but a little orthodox tea is also made.

Kenya leaf has a reddish-black appearance. The brew is dark, strong and hearty with earthy, smoky notes at times but usually without such subtleties. One imagines it is the perfect tea for trench warfare and other wholesome outdoor activities. I like the taste of the ancient African earth in it and for this reason often prefer it to Assam when a no-nonsense tea is what's called for. Kericho and Limuru are the favored growing districts in the Highlands, where Ragati, Kipkoimet and Marinym are among the best-known estates.

RUSSIA (THE CAUCASUS)

$\mathcal{W}$hat follows may be read as a requiem, for "Russian" tea may well be extinct. Even before war enveloped the lands of the Caucasus where it grew, the principal estates were irradiated in the aftermath of the Chernobyl disaster, which reportedly poisoned some 90 percent of the tea acreage in Georgia. Some tea was grown in Armenia and Azerbaijan also, but in light of all the uncertainties in the region, how much remains is anybody's guess. This is not the kind of glowing report one would like to give, for the former Soviet Union was a major tea producer with a fascinating history.

China tea plants have been cultivated in what is now the Republic of Georgia since 1848. Chakve, the largest and best-known estate in the former U.S.S.R., was originally a property of the Crown, planted in 1892. With over 200,000 acres under tea, all told, the country was estimated to produce about 330 million pounds of black tea a year. Most of this was grown on the hills overlooking the eastern shore of the Black Sea, a region where snow is not uncommon. It is (or was) the world's northernmost tea district and the only one to produce both tea and wine.

Production had been mechanized to some degree since the 1920s when a Russian named Sandovsky invented the world's first tea-plucking machine. Whatever the methods, the result was a handsome leaf of orthodox manufacture, always beautifully black and well twisted. This appearance was its major charm, unfortunately, for it yielded a somewhat light-colored, thin-bodied tea which tended to taste flat. To have not even such poor tea as this any longer must be an especially bitter thing to a Russian.

When the soil eventually recovers from the Chernobyl disaster, there's no reason the Caucasus should not produce rather splendid tea. For the foreseeable future, though, it's highly doubtful if any of the teas sold as "Russian" can honestly claim any such origin. It's not a bad thing, however, to keep a noble old name alive.

TURKEY

Travelers to Turkey don't need to be told about the unique flavor of Turkish *çay*, which one is offered almost immediately upon entering any premises there. Tea, the social lubricant of choice throughout Muslim societies, never tastes better than in Turkey. *Çay* sells a lot of carpets. Other teas may have an aftertaste, but with Turkish tea, "backlash" may be more to the point. *Çay* is a distinctly different black tea, fairly light colored and weedy, you might say, keeping in mind the kind of weeds Medea had available in that same corner of the Black Sea where it's now grown.

Turkish coffee became largely a memory at the end of World War I. Ataturk, the national savior, transformed the Turks into a nation of tea drinkers by ordering it planted and produced locally, starting in 1928. The tea seeds and plants came from neighboring Georgia, descendants of the small-leafed China bushes the czars had set out eighty years earlier. They were planted just a few kilometers across the border from Georgia around the town of Rize, a name you often see on Turkish tea packages.

Caykur, the government monopoly, today maintains forty-five plantations totaling 200,000 acres with an annual production of about 250 million pounds of tea. By my calculations, this amounts to more tea per Turk than even the Irish drink, and the Irish are Europe's leading tea consumers. Turkish women have developed a unique plucking method using special scissors. The Turks tax imported tea remorselessly and export as little as possible of their own. Only in Turkey, as a result, does tea-growing mean something other than poverty for the workers.

I find *çay* one of the world's most enjoyable teas, especially at the teahouse in the Topkapi Palace on Seraglio Point with a view of Istanbul's Golden Horn and the Bosporus beyond. I challenge you to try it there and disagree. And when I can find it, every sip takes me back. When I do return someday, I shall look into the matter of seasons, flushes and all the rest.

OTHER TEA LANDS

Tea is produced in over fifty countries worldwide, sad testimony to the grinding poverty of the Third World, for even if some of these countries gain a place in the world market, tea is a crop that guarantees only the barest subsistence to those who produce it.

Theoretically, at least, there is hope of locating another region with the potential greatness of Darjeeling, say, somewhere in the Andes, where Brazil, Ecuador, Bolivia and Peru have been setting out small, high-grown gardens. Argentina, with over 100,000 acres, is South America's largest producer. It is unarguably some of the poorest-quality tea produced anywhere, yet about one-fourth of U.S. imports in recent years have come from Argentina, destined for use as tea-bag filler. Equally poor tea now comes from Guatemala.

Tea is raised throughout East Africa, where it was first planted in Malawi in 1887. Much is now grown in Uganda, Zaire, Mozambique, Burundi, Cameroon, Rwanda and Tanzania—all of it black tea and utterly forgettable.

The island of Mauritius in the Indian Ocean has a reputation for reasonable quality. Its plantations have beautiful names like Chartreuse, Marie Anguilles and Corson. Corson Vanilla Tea has an international following.

Bangladesh has grown tea of fair quality since the nineteenth century in the Cachar and Sylhet districts next door to Assam, but almost all is for home consumption. The same goes for Iran's annual production of perhaps forty million pounds, grown on extensive estates near the Caspian Sea.

Vietnam, with a long history of tea production, has just begun shipping limited quantities of her top quality teas via Sri Lankan and American entrepreneurs to whom we owe thanks for a new experience, perhaps a new delight.

Classic Blends

The following descriptions are of the most popular tea blends, and some blenders are mentioned as examples which we have tasted. For a complete list of teas, tea blenders, tea shops and tea wholesalers, refer to our "Directory" chapter.

English Breakfast

Almost every American tea dealer and tea brand offers a tea blend by this name, a claim which cannot be made in England, by the way. "English Breakfast" is as meaningless as "California Burgundy"—it means whatever the blender wants it to. The claim that China Keemun is the "traditional" English Breakfast tea has no historical basis—the English had been drinking tea at breakfast for two hundred years by the time Keemun was first produced in the 1870s. Any combination of pungent, colory black teas intended as an eye-opener may be so called; though seldom very bad, it is seldom unusually good either.

Russian Caravan

Russia's caravan trade with China dates to a treaty of 1689 and continued growing in volume until the opening of the final links in the Trans-Siberian Railway. No

Russian alive today can remember the he-man smell of hot camel that old Russia's tea must have had from 1689 to 1900, when the last caravan carrying tea for Russia set out from Beijing. To compensate for this deficiency, tea merchants everywhere have long purveyed various blends intended to suggest those romantic days of caravans and samovars. Their blends naturally vary in composition and quality but are often quite distinguished. While many no longer use China black tea exclusively for this fantasy tea, tradition dictates a certain smokiness obtainable only from Lapsang Souchong, the one ingredient—in whatever proportion—all Russian Caravan blends seem to have in common.

Irish Breakfast

Different tea-drinking countries have distinctly different tastes: the Irish in particular illustrate this point. No people in Europe consume more tea per capita—or better. "The Irish Free State," observed tea authority W. H. Ukers in 1935, "always secures the choicest teas." Irish Breakfast tea is intended to capitalize on this cachet and tradition. It used to mean "mainly Assam," and outside of Ireland still does. Irish companies like Bewley's, Shamrock and McGraths increasingly use African teas in their blends, however, and from such stalwart blends one learns a new respect both for Irish taste and African tea. Teas of this style are meant to be very hearty and go best with milk.

Royalties

Ever since the marriage of tea lovers Charles II and Catherine of Braganza, the British have always associated their monarchy with tea and merchants have looked for ways to associate their teas with royalty. The practice reached its apex in the days of Victoria's "Buy Empire" campaigns, but the names of monarchs and the dear, if regrettably horsey, features of England's royal family continue to adorn tea canisters. Present-day protocol governing these things was explained to me by a director of Jacksons of Piccadilly:

> The rules are now very much stricter than they were at one time. If, for instance, we wanted to call a tea Princess of Wales blend, we would have to ask her permission through her secretary. I am told that nowadays this would not be

granted. . . . The Royal Family is very careful indeed not to link their names to commercial products and even if they ask for a particular blend, it is almost certain that they would not allow their names to be linked to it except through a Royal Warrant. If a trader regularly supplies the Royal Household with a particular product, e.g., Jacksons English Breakfast, for a minimum of three years, the company can apply for the grant of a Royal Warrant. But, if they cease to supply, the Warrant after a year or two may be withdrawn.

There is a story about King George V's butler which might amuse you. He had a number of teas in his pantry on a tray which got knocked off the table, and the teas were spilt on the floor. Being a lazy man, he swept them up and put them into a single box, and shortly afterward made tea for the King. He said it was the best tea he ever drank, and told the butler he never wanted any other. He went off to a tea blender and asked them to make up a matching blend and that company still supplies the Royal Household to this day. But, they do not use the name of the butler—or the King—as a brand name.

Most royal teas are nostalgically named, like Fortnum & Mason Queen Anne Tea, named in honor of their founders' patroness. Others are genuine relics: Ridgways still sells HMB (Her Majesty's Blend), a tea created for Victoria, as was Melrose Queen's Tea. The Canadian firm Murchie's, founded over a century ago by a former Melrose employee, still sells teas which John Murchie originally blended for Victoria and delivered in person to Balmoral castle.

O'Clock Teas

Along with "Breakfast," there are other generically named teas intended for other times of the day. It is a sign of the times that nobody markets a Bed Tea any longer, to be served before you rise for breakfast. The closest thing to it is the excellent and lightly scented Indar "Boudoir Tea," meant for whenever the opportunity arises, no doubt, and for years the only French tea sold in the United States. Jacksons sells its Afternoon and Evening teas in Victorian-style caddies, and an excellent Afternoon Tea is available from Murchie's. The Four O'Clock Tea Company was recently established by an Englishwoman, Angela Stevenson, who relocated to Connecticut, where she began importing teas to insure a source for her own "4 o'clocks." This veddy Brit thing of O'Clock teas manifests itself most fully in the only five teas which were ever sold by Tea Planters & Importers Company, London—Morning Tea, Lunchtime Tea, Afternoon Tea, Evening Tea and Drawing Room Tea.

Chai Masala

India, a comparative latecomer to tea, deserves undying thanks for the invention of *chai masala*, the "tea mixture" which seems to fuel the entire subcontinent. It is available in every village and on every street from *chaiwallas* (tea vendors) and may be made in varying strengths. Truck drivers, for instance, may be heard asking for "one-hundred-kilometer" or "five-hundred-kilometer" *chai*. The most prized is probably Kashmiri-style *chai*, which a secret ingredient turns a startling pink.

The preferred black tea for *chai* is Nilgiri, which *chaiwallas* know how to brew over and over again. Upon smelling an exceptionally fragrant Nilgiri, a friend who's been there recalled at once: "That's how *chai* smells in India!" The tea is boiled with milk and a pinch of soda and diverse spices, crushed cardamom seeds above all. While the *chai* boils, it is constantly stirred and poured by the ladleful through the air. The makings for this exotic and sublime concoction are available in the United States from India Tea Importers and our own nascent *chaiwallas* like Live Chai, Oregon Chai or Chai Brewers of Santa Cruz, California. One taste and one hopes it will soon be available everywhere.

Bunting Original Ostfriesen Tea

The people inhabiting the coast of the North Sea between Holland and Denmark are called Frisian, as is the language they speak, which is distinct from Dutch and German and said to be the closest linguistic cousin to English. When the Dutch brought the first tea to Europe in the early 1600s, they promptly began selling this exotic novelty to their quasi-German, coastal-dwelling neighbors.

Long before tea became England's national habit, the Ostfriesen (to give them their modern name) made tea a national luxury and established a trade which has kept them supplied with the world's finest teas to this day. It is due to this trade that Hamburg and Bremen eclipsed London as the tea capitals of Europe, and Germany has become the most quality-conscious tea market in the world. Germany purchases approximately 80 percent of the annual Darjeeling crop, reexporting a great deal but consuming most of the finest. Although the Ostfriesen made up less than 2 percent of the former West Germany's population, they alone consumed 25 percent of the country's tea.

The Ostfriesen typically have a cup of tea immediately after rising, more with breakfast, again at eleven A.M., and at least once every afternoon and evening. It's no wonder they have developed tea customs all their own and pride themselves on tea connoisseurship. The most popular Ostfriesen tea today is from the House of Bunting, and is one of the oldest tea concerns in Europe. The firm has sold its Original Ostfriesen Tea since 1806, the blend evolved gradually over the years. Bunting now specializes in extraordinary Assams, which they blend with other top-quality teas to create an exceptionally rich, aromatic and full-bodied brew, unreservedly recommended. It is intended to be drunk the Ostfriesen way, with boulders of crystallized sugar called *Kluge* crackling in the bottom of the cup and a cloud of unstirred milk through which you sip the tea. Any Ostfriesen tea is sure to be excellent.

Proprietary Blends

Proprietary names are used to designate a merchant's unique or favorite tea blends: **Fortnum & Mason's Fortmason**, for example, which is a specially scented China-India blend. The oldest tea purveyor in Greenwich Village, New York—**Schapira's**—sells a wonderful Flavor Cup Ceylon Tea "served by our family for over seventy years." Murchie's of Canada has wonderfully interesting nineteenth-century blends, sometimes of green and black teas, and examples from other firms abound. Many clubs, hotels and restaurants, and even many individuals, have long maintained private blends of tea.

An old-time custom that tea dealers still observe today is to keep a file of their regular customers' personal blends, exactly which teas and in what proportions. One can always go to the merchant and obtain somebody else's blend, but never the recipe, which is kept in strictest confidence. Such blends are naturally named after the customer, and not a few of them have been widely popularized when said customer happened to have as many friends or envious enemies as Lady Londonderry or Earl Grey. There were also blends merchants made for specific markets—Fortnum & Mason still sells a Dowager Tea. Though Nursery Tea or Invalid Tea are nowhere to be found, they were ubiquitous in Victoria's day—Ty-phoo originated as an Invalid Tea.

Maryland's **Eastern Shore Tea Company** has thirty or more proprietary blends, and most other companies have one or several—the list would be impressive. A good number of these deserve a place among the *grands seigneurs* like those I love most and will describe below. It is manifestly unfair to omit them, and ignorance is my only excuse. Your pantry shelf may well include other proprietary teas of equal distinction with mine, but these are the best of those I have discovered to date, and some of them, at least, are sure to please you too.

Boston Harbour Tea—"Bawstonaba Registered Trademark" is still a British export of Davison, Newman & Company, Ltd., a London firm which was already 127 years old when Messrs. Davison and Newman gave it their names in 1777. It was tea of theirs that was tipped overboard in Boston a few years previously, and the tins today reproduce their petition to the Crown for compensation. The business had been founded in 1650 by one Rawlinson, a tavern-keeper friend of Samuel Pepys. Only two other British firms can trace their history back this far. This excellent tea goes far toward making amends for its name.

Drysdales Connoisseur Blend—This powerfully aromatic and complex nectar may be the Anglo-Saxon ideal of a black tea blend, a Scottish sort of luxury. So astringent it affects parts of my mouth I'd forgotten, it demands exactly three minutes' steeping—any longer and it's unforgivingly undrinkable. Finely powdered, quick-infusing, and made for milk and sugar, it even welcomes cream: spirits optional. The blend was created by a small family firm founded in Edinburgh in 1878 and still famous for quality tea.

Grace Owners Blend—The only problem with Grace Rare Teas is deciding which one to single out for praise. For those with a taste for the bitter, there is Grace Demitasse Tea, primarily fine Assam and Darjeeling with exotic leaves added to harmonize body and flavor. Another nonpareil is Grace Connoisseur Blend, a somewhat eccentric faithful friend, and how could anyone praise Grace Winey Keemun adequately? "Owners Blend," writes owner Richard Sanders, "is an English Breakfast patterned after our Winey Keemun, which is primarily China Keemun that's balanced each year with other Keemun-style teas plus several from India. The formula varies from five to seven teas depending on crop quality. The blend is given added body, subtle overtones and aroma enhancement from a significant amount of Yunnan and a mild jolt from high-grown Ceylon, a Nuwara Eliya. While its general character is 'English Breakfast,' it is our best all-around tea."

J. P. Morgan Tea—A man of wealth and taste whose name remains famous though most of us know nothing about him, Mr. Morgan—as his Library attests—was a lover of art and books who cherished peace and quiet—and tea. There was a tea firm near his offices which Mr. Morgan walked past for years, and he always saw the same taster at work, "sipping, spitting and looking wise," as it's been described. One day he ventured inside for this professional's appraisal of his personal blend. He left, the story goes, visibly agitated and shouting, "What do you know about tea?" The magisterial taster maintained his look of mild authority until the financier was out of sight and then broke into gales of laughter. "Now that ought to bother him the rest of his life: He's got the best tea money can buy, and I called it the worst I'd ever tasted!"

Mr. Morgan's is one of the more interesting blends, certainly, as many-layered as it is harmonious. Central to the flavor is the rounded, fruity taste of Formosa oolong, to which is married the astringent character of various black teas. Binding and suffusing both tastes and aromas is a faint smokiness from Lapsang Souchong. One would never imagine Lapsang could play such an understated role or impart such elegance.

This remarkable achievement of the blender's art was created by Mr. Morgan and Lester Vail in the 1920s. Simpson & Vail, a firm which has been an institution for New York tea lovers for over ninety years, still sells the blend, which is also available at the Morgan Library.

Lady Londonderry Blend—Lady Londonderry ordered this blend of Ceylon, India and Formosa teas to be prepared for her by Jacksons of Piccadilly throughout the first quarter of this century, when she was London's most famous hostess. Its popularity spread like that of a contemporary example I might mention, the Imogen Cunningham blend which my own dealer, Freeds, concocted to the exact specifications of the late photographer. Freeds often supplied her numerous friends with it and now—even though Imogen is absent—her tea keeps winning new friends and gaining popularity. Getting back to Lady Londonderry, her taste in tea was likewise quite good.

Palm Court Blend—A tea I hope never to run out of, this masterpiece was created for Harney & Son by William MacMelville, one of the tea industry's most respected gurus. Some may never enjoy J. P. Morgan tea for the perfectly understandable reason that they cannot abide Lapsang Souchong—tastes differ—but it's hard to imagine a black tea lover who does not fall in love with Harney's Palm Court Blend. It combines four teas, but beyond a little oolong and a strong suggestion of Ceylon, there's no telling which. Nothing is faint about this mouth-filling taste with its note of ripe figs. It is a tea as lush as the surroundings for which it was designed, the Palm Court at the Plaza, New York's premier gathering place for afternoon tea, where it's served as the house blend.

China Moon Blend—This is an entirely different species of masterpiece created not for afternoon tea *à l'anglaise* but to accompany the imaginative modern Chinese cuisine of Barbara Tropp's celebrated China Moon Cafe in San Francisco. Here is no solo performance but a symphony of green, oolong and black teas, with simple-seeming yet surprisingly complex flavors. For those who insist, it even accommodates milk and sugar—just don't ask for this in Miss Tropp's restaurant! Another creation by Augie Techeira of Freed Teller & Freed's.

Shanghai Nights—Tea master Roy Fong of Imperial Tea Court, San Francisco, was inspired by the lively brightly lit bustle of cosmopolitan Shanghai to weave these tastes together from a blend of China teas nobody has ever before thought to combine. It fuses into a subtle, seamless flavor which fairly sings in the mouth. Friends often exclaim this is the best tea they've ever tasted.

Lipton's Yellow Label—Thomas J. Lipton, Inc., which is generally believed to sell over half the tea consumed in the United States, has always been a separate company from the mother firm in England, and a similar arrangement applies with Lipton's in India. Its rich-tasting CTC (cut-tear-curl) blend in a garish yellow package is labeled in English and Arabic: "Manufactured in India by Lipton Export Division of Hindustan Lever Ltd., Bombay by arrangement with the Trade Mark Proprietors Lipton Limited."

The box holds 450 grams (about a pound) and retails in Indo-Pakistani groceries for perhaps five dollars. The tea is good reason enough to hunt down one of these ethnic outlets. I love and respect this CTC, described as "a selection of high-grade Indian teas carefully chosen for their strength and delicious flavor." Every word of it true—this is black tea of pachyderm strength and proportions, which serves to illustrate what poor stuff almost all other mass market teas really are. Our American Lipton's, for what it's worth, ranks with the "best" of these, which include:

Salada, a Kellogg product, is about the only U.S. example one hears tea professionals mention with respect. **Ty-phoo** is another somewhat-above-average blend, and New Zealand's **Bell Tea** is not half bad.

Scented, Spiced and Flavored Teas

Earl Grey—Earl Grey commemorates the second Grey to bear the title of earl, which is a rank in the English peerage above viscount and below marquess—a count, in any other language. In his politics Charles Earl Grey (1764–1845) was the humane and energetic Whig rival of the arch-Tory Duke of Wellington, whom he bested to become prime minister for a short time in the 1830s. Besides much else, he deserves eternal credit for the abolition of slavery throughout the British Empire, but it's for his favorite tea that he is remembered.

Mystery surrounds the origins of Earl Grey tea. One story has it he was already drinking it before becoming prime minister, having personally received the recipe from a mandarin while serving as a diplomat in China. According to another account, he got this recipe from China indirectly, only after leaving office. Either way is strange enough, for the Chinese are not and never have been drinkers of Earl Grey. The mystery only deepened when competing English firms laid claim to the "original" Earl Grey formula. An heiress to Jacksons of Picadilly long ago claimed: "This [secret recipe] was entrusted by Lord Grey to George Charlton in 1830— who was a partner of Robert Jackson and Company—Jacksons remains sole proprietors of this original formula which remains unaltered today. There are many imitations but none match Jacksons original blend."

Twinings, the other contender, calls it merely "an error in merchandising" that neither the earl nor the Twining family patented the name. Twinings tins bear this ambiguous message from the present earl: "Legend has it that my ancestor, the second Earl Grey, was presented with this exquisite recipe by an envoy on his return from China. Generations of my family have enjoyed Earl Grey tea and, today, I am proud to continue this tradition with the tea celebrated throughout the world known as Twinings Earl Grey Tea." Considering that no Darjeeling tea was even planted until eleven years after the good earl's death, it is quite a mystery how Twinings's "original" formula employs "long leaf China and Darjeeling teas." Now that Twinings has acquired Jacksons, however, this 150-year-old controversy has no doubt been dropped.

To some, the real mystery about Earl Grey tea is how did a tea that's nice enough now and then get to be an international bestseller? Not that we actively dislike the stuff, mind you—it has its place and gives its pleasures too—but why on earth are multitudes crazy about it? "I have a theory," Samuel H. G. Twining, OBE, says of Twinings's tremendous sales of Earl Grey in over ninety countries. "People often suffer from what I call a tortured and twisted palate after too much coffee drinking and do not appreciate ordinary teas and yet enjoy a more definite flavor such as Earl Grey." Could be he's onto something.

What makes Earl Grey taste the way it does, regardless of the source or sort of tea used, is the oil of bergamot with which it's scented. Earl Grey was the first scented tea drunk in the West, as far as I know, and its popularity with us parallels that of Jasmine tea in China. Bergamot, by the way, has nothing to do with the town of Bergamo in Italy. It is a Turkish name given a pear-shaped fruit (*Citrus bergamia*) long grown around the Mediterranean for the oil that can be pressed out of its rind for use in perfumery, and nowadays chiefly in Earl Grey tea. The source and amount of bergamot used determines the intensity of scent, which varies widely from one tea to the next.

Jasmine—Jasmine is by far the world's most popular scented tea and by far the most and the best of it comes from China. The Chinese classify it into seven different grades or "quality standards" and also produce a limited amount of "Extra Fancy." The poorest can be foul tasting, but the uncommon delicacy of superb Jasmine like Yin Hao is an instant reminder of the joys of life. The top grades are teas of great subtlety, perfectly wedding fragrance and flavor. Like many another sophisticate, Ian Fleming's James Bond is a Yin Hao devotee. But Yin Hao itself pales in comparison with the limited-production Jasmine types Chinese know, for example, Tailao, or "Grandmother Jasmine." Green or Pouchong are the base teas used; the spent flowers may or may not be removed but contribute only visual appeal in any case. Jasmine is a good accompaniment to most chicken dishes and many desserts; the Chinese traditionally drink it with spicy and strong-tasting foods.

The jasmine shrub (*Jasminium sambac*) is native to the Persian Gulf area and was brought to south China sometime before the third century A.D. Under the Ming dynasty, the Chinese developed a passion for flowers regardless of variety, shape or color, and green tea scented with fresh flowers became a court favorite. Within a few generations, however, it had grown so universally popular that the upper classes began to disdain it as "servants' tea." It remains the most popular kind of tea throughout northern China. It was only introduced to the West during the nineteenth century.

China produces Jasmine tea in seven provinces, at least, but the best comes from around Fuzhou in Fujian. (Just across the Straits, Taiwan also produces notable Jasmine.) "Before-the-rains" green tea, plucked from early April to late May, is steamed—only steamed leaf absorbs scent well—and stored until August, when the blazing summer brings the jasmine into flower. Blossoms are picked when most tightly closed, around noon; as the temperature cools in the evening, they begin to burst open (with a faint popping sound), and the scenting operation begins. Nowadays flowers and tea are mixed in machines which control temperature and humidity. While lower grades are scented just two or three times, the best receive five to seven repetitions, using twice as much jasmine as tea. To prevent molding, the tea must then be refired to remove the flowers' moisture; sometimes the dried blooms from the last scenting are not removed. The popularity of the jasmine fragrance has led to a wonderful variety of teas, from superb to extraordinary and from ordinary to mediocre. Let your palate be your guide.

Jasmine Pearl—extraordinary hand-rolled pellets (beware of imitations); Tailao and other unobtainable superlatives

Yin Hao (Silver Down) Jasmine—Highest Standard Extra-Fancy, FS901

Chung Feng (Spring Wind) Jasmine—Superb Extra-Fancy, FS902

Chung Hao (Spring Down)—Extra-Fancy FS904

Restaurant Grade—by way of contrast—is usually Standard, FS906 or FS907

Lapsang Souchong—This might be called "a man's tea." Lapsang is probably the most assertive of all black teas, with a character, like that of Scotch whiskey, which you either love or detest on its own not-uncertain terms. Like Scotch, its principal characteristic is a smokiness which may vary from one example to the next but which always rises to greet you as soon as you open the canister. China's Fujian province and Taiwan are the only places in the world which produce it. Formosa Souchong generally has a grayish tinge and includes a good deal of stem. Chinese is black as homemade sin, free of stems and rather more tightly twisted. Both yield a rich red brew that's almost syrupy and an aroma you couldn't miss in a high wind.

Without making an outright claim, the head of one august London tea firm has hinted that his Lapsang Souchong is the queen's favorite tea. That great lover of Lapsang, Sir Winston Churchill, added Scotch whiskey to his. Devotees accept no substitute once they've latched onto the precise brand they prefer. Mark T. Wendell's justly famous Hu-Kwa brand of Lapsang makes up over half the firm's direct mail business. Chinese connoisseurs neither recognize the name nor drink the tea; it seems to be made strictly for export on an obscure Wu-I mountain called Puon Shan. The tea is cured like a ham in rooms filled with pinewood smoke, which impregnates and does not simply coat the leaf.

Lichee Tea—Variously spelled, lichee is usually thought a nut in the West because of its tough, woody skin, but it is really a fruit from an evergreen tree (*Litchi chinensis.*) It is one of south China's most famous fruits, in fact, and its flesh has been likened to white jade for smoothness and color. When fresh and juicy, it has succulent texture and a sweet-tart taste a little reminiscent of grapefruit. For over a thousand years this perishable delicacy has also been known in Chinese as Feizi Xiao, or "Feizi's Smile." The story is that one of the Tang emperors was madly in love with his concubine Feizi, who is celebrated as one of the four most famous beauties in Chinese history. To make her happy, the emperor had fresh lichee, her favorite fruit, brought to his capital by relays of horsemen riding day and night. Sad to say, his infatuation eventually caused him to lose his throne and Feizi as well. Feizi's Smile belongs to the soapberry family, botanically speaking. From the taste of canned lichee, one judges it wellnamed. Lichee tea is a China black flavored with the fresh juice of this exotic fruit. It is among the few black teas the Chinese seem to enjoy.

Rose Tea—This China tea is scented in much the same way as Jasmine, one supposes, with the difference that the base tea used is black. From a rose's point of view, it must seem that the whole point of human civilization has been to multiply its petals. The rose the ancient Romans praised had no more than four to six petals, and one must assume its cousin in ancient China was no better endowed.

As roses with more and more colors and odor and complexity were developed, they began to be used in perfumes, sauces, condiments and, eventually, tea. According to scholar John C. Evans, this tea originated in Hunan province under the flower-

loving Ming dynasty. "Originally only the petals of the 'tea rose' (*Rosa odorata*) were used. This native Chinese 'half-hardy' bush-rose has large tea-scented blossoms, whence the name. Unfortunately, petals from tea roses are not always used and some rose congous smell like a bouquet of roses instead of tea."

Exotics—The Chinese scent green, oolong and black teas, and often employ flowers unknown to us, or at least to me. *Bailan*—magnolia— I know, but then there's *chulan* (chloranthus), *daidai*, *youtze* (pomelo), *Milan* and osmanthus, a rare flower used in some of the world's most famous fragrances. Osmanthus tea is black but has the body and astringency of a green tea with a light fruity flavor. As for the others, who knows where to buy them?

Spiced Teas and "Constant Comment"—The practice of spicing tea, like adding water to whiskey, though deplorable, is something people have done throughout history. In the late 1930s Ruth Campbell Bigelow began packaging a spiced tea in her home. When she introduced it on the national market in 1944, sealed in little black jars, she called it Constant Comment. Its success made the R. C. Bigelow Company a major tea firm in the United States, and its depredations continue unabated. All that needs to be said about any spiced tea is written on the label—if it says Orange and Clove Spiced Tea, that's exactly what it will taste like. The tea itself would be an insult to mediocrity in many—perhaps most—cases, but that does not detract from the pleasure it can give under the right circumstances. Besides, spiced tea is not created with lovers of the leaf in mind, but for people who want a hot, spicy beverage. To each his peach.

Flavored Teas—To each his peach, continued: Flavored teas are now said to account for roughly one-third of all specialty tea sales. Thinking back, this is also how tea drinking began, since the most ancient types of tea were flavored, early tea being a far cry from the delicious drink it is today. To make it taste less bitter and medicinal, one of China's earliest tea writers said, "add onion, ginger and orange to flavor." Lu Yu, writing centuries later, mentions jujube fruit, dogwood berries, and peppermint, as flavorings, adding, purist that he was, "Drinks like that are no more than the swill of gutters and ditches; still, alas, it is a common practice to make teas that way." The loose-leaf tea we know has been widely used only a little over five hundred years, since around the time the Ming dynasty was founded in 1368. If the flower-obsessed Ming went on to invent scented tea, it was left to twentieth-century technology to provide flavored teas of the kind popularized since the 1970s.

It has long been appreciated that tea is perhaps nature's finest flavor medium, always ready to absorb and carry in its pores many another taste. Tea shippers and merchants have always struggled to guard their precious products against off-odors, and sooner or later every tea lover discovers just how ever-present this danger is. A minor mishap or inattention can give you a garlic or coriander tea if the leaf was even momentarily exposed to cooking odors, say. I once created basil tea (which wasn't half bad) in this way. But recent decades have seen the full range of flavoring explored not by accident by design.

It is devoutly to be hoped that the current fad for flavored teas will lead Americans to the discovery of tea *au naturel.* The flavored wines of the sixties are given much credit for launching this country's boom in wine drinking; before them, winos made up the majority of American wine consumers. To a confirmed tea lover, these soda pop teas are a kind of Kool-Aid, and it's hard at first not to react like a wine connoisseur who's been handed a glass of Boone's Farm. If one can manage to be open-minded, it becomes possible to imagine a place for flavored teas in their own right. They can be very pleasant dessert teas, for one thing. Chocolate anything will fight ordinary tea and win, but pair it with Boysenberry or Gooseberry tea from Royal Gardens and you have a marriage made in heaven. Simpson & Vail sells a Kiwi-Watermelon tea I find quite appealing iced. There must be others with beautiful balance and wonderfully subtle fruit flavors like these, but I lay no claim to wide experience and see no need to catalog the flavors available.

Halssen & Lyon, the giant tea firm in Hamburg, Germany, undoubtedly produces most of the world's flavored tea. Modern technology can be used not only to extract naturally occurring essences but also to duplicate them artificially, and artificial flavors are usually found to work better than natural ones because they are more intense. Not all teas take well to flavoring, which seems to work best with certain Ceylons and China blacks. In any case, the tea used is almost always undistinguished, to say the least, and can be Vile Stuff. But who are we to argue with a mass market for every flavor from apricot to ylang-ylang?

Part 2

A Brief History of Tea

The gastronomic arts are a huge field, the borders of which are constantly being pushed back by every person who makes them the object of serious study or profound thought. These arts embrace all three realms of nature, and the four corners of the globe, all moral considerations and all social relationships. Everything comes within their scope in a more or less direct way, and if they may seem superficial, it is only to vulgar minds, who see no more to a kitchen than saucepans and no more to dinner than dishes.

—Grimod de La Reyniere *L'Almanach des Gourmands*, 1803

Tea is a consciousness-altering substance obtained from the leaves of an evergreen shrub, *Camellia sinensis*, which has been in continuous use since the pyramids were built. Its fascinating and neglected history brings together a mass of things we half know already in a way that gives an entirely new perspective on the history of the last five hundred years to go no further. It is strange to discover a single plant at the root of many forces shaping history. To learn its story makes it impossible to look at our world in quite the same way again.

Legends shroud the origins of tea. The most widely repeated of these attributes its discovery to Shen Nung, an emperor said to have ruled China around 2700 B.C.

In other stories, tea was brought to China from India by a Buddhist monk named Gan Lu about the time of Christ, or sprouted from the severed eyelids of the patriarch of Zen, Bodhidharma, five hundred years later in China. Historians say many Chinese tea customs can be traced as far back as the Zhou dynasty, which ended in 222 B.C. It is mentioned in this period by Confucius (551–479 B.C.), who knew tea by the name *tu*. Tea was called by other names also, but *tu* became *te*, the word in Fujian dialect which Europeans eventually learned and carried around the world. *Chai*, as tea is called in India, Russia and throughout Central Asia, must come from *cha-i*, Chinese for "tea leaves."

Cha, the distinctive ideogram by which tea is presently known in China, first appeared in an herbal written about A.D. 725 during the Tang dynasty. By this time the plant had spread over most of China's present-day growing area, and the drink had been widely used for well over one thousand years. Since A.D. 476 it had been a commodity that the Chinese bartered with nomadic barbarians beyond the Wall in exchange for horses. Despite abundant references by one name or another, tea became the subject of a book for the first time when Lu Yu wrote *Cha Ching*, or *Tea Encyclopedia*, about A.D. 780. This same year, the Tang emperor levied the first tea tax, proof positive that tea had become big business.

Tea as we know it today took a long, slow time evolving. It began as a medicine, no doubt, and gradually came to be taken as a tonic, and after that as a drink. By Lu Yu's day the leaf was made into cakes which had to be powdered and roasted by a "tea master," who alone knew how to boil up a perfect brew. Lu Yu described twenty-four different implements and utensils developed by trial and error over the centuries in Buddhist monasteries and the palaces of the wealthy, needed to accomplish this ritual. Lu Yu's book was probably commissioned by people in the tea business, and the ritual he prescribed is secular and not religious. All the same, an indefinable spirituality clung to his procedures and attitudes toward tea, and this has persisted in every culture which has adopted the drink ever since.

Following Tang times, the Song dynasty (960–1279) abandoned boiling and developed a new way of making cake tea by whipping the powdered leaf in hot water with a bamboo whisk. This called for different wares, utensils and procedures. Among the other Song innovations were Tribute Teas, earmarked for the emperor and every year transported by relays of horses to ensure they arrived perfectly fresh. Whereas the favorite Tang teas had come from Zhejiang province, the forty-one Song Tribute Teas were all produced in Fujian, many of them "cliff teas" from the Wu-I mountains, later to become known to the West as Bohea. Chinese villagers drank only the tea they produced locally, but by Song times the urban market for fine teas of diverse origin included perhaps twenty million cultured and literate customers.

The Song poet-emperor Huizong (who ruled from 1100 to 1125) wrote a treatise on tea in which he singled out as the rarest and finest of all a white tea from Fujian, a type of tea which has only in our times ever been seen outside China. At a less exalted level, the Song era saw the eclipse of the "tea master" and the spread of tea-houses throughout China as a variety of teas became affordable for all.

Tea had been introduced to Japan long before the Song era but was not grown there. In about 1200 A.D., a Japanese monk named Eisei, returning from studies in Mainland China, brought back tea plants and Zen. The two have been inextricably linked in the Japanese mind ever since; as their popular proverb says, "The flavor of tea and the flavor of Zen are the same." Eisei wrote the first Japanese book on tea, and the plants he gave to his friend and fellow monk, Myo-E, still flourish where they were planted at Uji near Kyoto. Also preserved in Japan to this day is the Song method of preparing tea, which became the basis for *chanoyu*, the Japanese tea ceremony.

The Song way of tea perished along with the nobility who practiced it during the period when the Mongols overran China. Marco Polo, who served in official capacities under Kublai Khan, never mentions tea at all in his travelogue. (He also omits any mention of the Great Wall, kites, printing and gunpowder.) When the Mongol dynasty was finally expelled in 1388 by the Ming in a national uprising, writers could no longer remember the various uses of the old-style tea implements. About the time Columbus was discovering the New World in the West, a new epoch in the history of this ancient drink was dawning in the Orient.

Innovations in processing the tea leaf had largely replaced older methods, so that under the Ming dynasty, for the first time, most tea was made in the loose-leaf form we know today. Tea makers also learned the secrets of oxidizing, misnamed "fermentation," which led to the discovery of oolong and black teas. And in order to prepare the new-style loose-leaf teas, potters and porcelain makers came up with the first teapots and the classic covered cup, used both to brew and serve tea, which is called a *guywan* in Mandarin (or *zhong* in Cantonese). The earliest teapots made at Yixing, where they are still produced, date to about 1492.

The 1500s witnessed the earliest direct contacts between European sea rovers and the Chinese, a Portuguese pirate having established himself at Macao as early as 1518. Over the following century first the Dutch and then the English wrested the China trade away from the Portuguese. Missionaries and adventurers wrote accounts of the wealth and ways of fabled Cathay, spreading knowledge of tea to Europe. It was not until 1610, however, that the first small sample of tea reached the Netherlands. At first this exotic luxury was confined to the aristocrats and the Dutch royal family, the House of Orange. (This probably accounts for that strange wedding of the words "Orange," originally a town in Provence, with the Chinese for "white down," *pa-ko*, which became "pekoe," which is still current in tea jargon as "Orange Pekoe.") From 1637 onward, the Dutch East India Company routinely imported tea on each vessel returning to Europe. They began selling it to their Frisian, French and, finally, English neighbors.

Tea was first sold in England by Thomas Garraway, a coffeehouse proprietor, in 1658, the same year Oliver Cromwell died. Diarist Samuel Pepys records his first taste of "the Chinean drink" in 1660, the same year the merry monarch Charles II was restored to the throne. He brought with him a taste for tea acquired during his exile at The Hague in Holland. With the aid of his Portuguese bride, Catherine of Braganza, whose dowry included chests of tea, the drink was made fashionable in the highest society. The English East India Company began imports of its own, and by 1676 its tea sales in London amounted to some ninety-four thousand pounds sterling.

By 1700, Chinese goods were no longer novelties in England but commodities in ever-increasing demand. Along with tea and silk came China's other great gift to this world, "china" itself. Hundreds of tons of this hitherto unimaginable ware had reached Europe as ballast in returning vessels. To trim the ship and make her sail properly, about half the weight had to be below the waterline as ballast, while tea and silk were stored higher to avoid water damage. It has been calculated that about sixty tons of porcelain were transported in this way for every thousand tons of tea. Because there was no kind of European pottery at this time which could withstand boiling water, the introduction of porcelain was critical to the spread of tea drinking in Europe.

It seems to be history's joke on Europe, England especially, that Chinese tea should become the world's first internationally traded commodity, imported over halfway round the globe, supporting a huge industry which probably accounted for 10 percent of England's gross national product, and giving rise to the most powerful multinational conglomerate the world has ever seen, the English East India Company. Yet, while all this was happening during the first three centuries of its use, nobody knew anything about how tea was grown, processed or blended or anything about the plant it came from.

China's only interest in foreign devils was to keep them at a safe distance. Brick tea, resembling the Tang-era cakes, was made in ever larger amounts for the age-old caravan trade with the peoples of Tibet and the nomads of Central Asia. China's new Manchu rulers, having overthrown the Ming dynasty in 1644, adopted a policy of restricting all other contact with foreigners to designated trade centers. The English and a few others were allowed access to the single port of Canton, while an *entrepôt* for the caravan trade was established on the Mongolian border for the less trouble-some Russians. Since Japan preserved a proud isolation, there was nowhere else on earth to buy tea, and the Chinese demanded cash payment in silver.

Though manageable in 1700, when England imported perhaps fifty tons of tea, by the 1760s England's annual tea imports amounted to some eighteen thousand tons, if one includes the probable quantity which was smuggled. This was simply too much to pay for every year in cash, and the Chinese had no use for British woolens or other goods. When the British-owned "Honorable Company" seized most of the Indian subcontinent, however, another article of commerce was found; in 1776 it shipped sixty tons of Indian opium to China. By 1790 the figure was three hundred tons, and the Honorable Company was well established as the first international narcotics cartel. By the time the company lost its monopoly on the China trade in 1834, it was shipping over three thousand tons of opium annually. Corrupt Chinese dealers paid for this contraband in silver, which was in turn applied to tea purchases on the spot. The tea purchased in this way was praised back in England by Methodist John Wesley and other "teetotalers" for making universal sobriety possible!

"In India, the British Empire was acquired in a fit of absence of kind," Winston Churchill once wrote, and might have added, because their thoughts were centered on getting to China. The history of the British raj is also a chapter in the history of tea, which is rich with such ripping yarns. The Boston Tea Party, leading to the American Revolution, is one of the best known, but there are many others: The history of the Russian caravan trade explains why the tea of that name tastes as it does. The story of tea in Japan alone could be a lifetime study. Then there's the discovery of the secret of making porcelain by a German alchemist at Dresden, and social developments as reflected in tea manners and wares in various cultures around the world. Like the inevitable Opium Wars of the 1840s, which completed the ruin of China, each of these topics deserves a book unto itself. This thumbnail account can attempt little more than to mention them. Yet the teas drunk round the world every day cannot be explained or understood except as monuments of a sort, living relics, of these past events and circumstances.

Tea history lives on in the cups before us. The proprietor of a "Houqua Mixture" at one time was a certain Captain Pidding, the Englishman remembered for having paid the then world-record price for eight chests of tea in January 1839, at the London tea auction. These historic chests contained the first tea ever sold in England that did not come from China but from Assam in India. Within the year, an Assam Company had been established and the India tea rush was on. Today, of course, India is the world's leading producer (and consumer) of tea—but that is another story.

"There is a great deal of poetry and fine sentiment in a chest of tea," Emerson wrote. Ceylon, Kenyan, Russian, etc.—there is not a tea you can ask for which does not bear witness to strange and wonderful stories, if only one cares to discover them. Turkish tea, for example, never existed before Ataturk decreed its cultivation in order to make the Turks the tea-drinking people they are today, because Mocha, the source of Turkish coffee, had been irretrievably lost with Arabian independence and the fall of the Ottoman Empire.

We are what we drink, no less than what we eat, and except for water, tea is the most widely consumed beverage in the world today. Yet less than four hundred years ago it was unheard of outside of China and its immediate vicinity. This is just as Isaac Disraeli, father of the famous Benjamin, foretold in 1790: "The progress of this famous plant has been something like the progress of truth; suspected at first, though very palatable to those who had the courage to taste it; resisted as it encroached; abused as its popularity seemed to spread; and establishing its triumph at last, in cheering the whole land from the palace to the cottage, only by the slow and restless efforts of time and its own virtues."

Tea Ceremonies: How to Prepare Tea

✖ ✖

Directions for tea making exemplify the difference between vocational training and education. George Orwell devoted one of his better essays to the subject, setting down precise directions, with a wealth of detailed admonishments as codicil, the whole expressing a sound philosophy, like the man himself. Orwell's "A Nice Cup of Tea" is an accomplishment greater than the catechism of the strong tea he relished, a little desperately, I feel, but relished heartily. And perhaps that's it—you have to put your heart into making tea if following the directions is to amount to much. Tea making is a ceremony which, like the drink itself, warms the heart somehow.

How to make tea—how, indeed? English, Frisian, Chinese or Kashmiri? With a samovar, a bamboo whisk, a kung-fu pot, a mug? You begin to see the dimensions here: ceremonies of sociability or family warmth, or, privately, of solitary solace and individual comfort. One thing all ways of making tea have in common is that each of them can be reduced to rules. That's the vocational training aspect. But information is not knowledge, and knowledge is not understanding—that is the fruit of time and education. But I digress, when I should be giving directions.

THE BLACK TEA CEREMONY

*T*he English afternoon-tea style of making tea is for black tea, suitable for larger groups. The point is refreshment—abundant tea as hot as possible as long as possible, and ease of replenishment. Always use forgiving, no-fuss teas that mistreatment cannot make undrinkable, for mistreatment is what this tradition teaches, unless one resorts to untraditional devices.

Boil water, warm pot, measure tea (plus a big one for the pot, traditionally)—the usual black tea procedure up to the fork in the road, at which you either (1) place loose tea in pot; or (2) place loose tea in a tea ball, sock or infusion basket for easy removal.

The first is the acceptable, traditional method, and any ill consequences which befall the tea are accepted in passing but ignored. When the pot is empty or almost so, or when the undrunk tea in it becomes stewy and oversteeped, boiling or even less-than-boiling water is added. Theoretically, the second steeping need not be inferior to the first, but it seldom seems to work out that way. Ideally, at least, the excess "tannin," if diluted, allows the weaker liquor of the secondary steeping to retain good bite and brightness without contributing bitterness. A joke about a Scotsman in the tea trade escaped me until I understood this. Of a tea he approved, the stingy Scot would say, "Aye, it takes a firm grip on the third water."

In practice, the tea is never as good as it could be when made this traditional English afternoon-tea way. It's always amused me that a leading practitioner, Mr. Samuel Twining, goes about opposing the use of a tea cosy, which he swears stews the tea instead of steeping it. Assuming Mr. Twining is right about the cosy, which I doubt, he never forbids going on to stew the tea anyway by oversteeping, at which point he blithely adds water, as if to wash away the sin. Though this works, the trouble is it does not work very well, not if the tea has any delicacy to lose.

More particular English tea drinkers used to decant the tea at its peak of perfection into a second, preheated pot. Handling a volume of scalding water sufficient for a large gathering can be daunting without servants. Even within an intimate circle, the maneuver requires a measure of grace not to seem strenuous, or even dangerous. Since the tea is less important than the food, conversation and camaraderie, however, this is usually seen as an unnecessary bother. There's no great loss, given England's typical milk-and-sugar-type black tea—most of the English have forgotten there's any other.

Placing the loose tea in a tea ball, sock, or infusion basket, the path seldom taken, unfailingly produces far better tea and therefore encourages drinking teas of real distinction and nuance. You remove leaf from liquor instead of vice versa. Unlike decanting, this requires no ungainly Herculean effort—you simply pluck the tea ball or other container out and into a waiting receptacle. Brewing time apart, you have here two main considerations: (1) making sure the leaf has room to expand fully in the infusion device you use, and (2) figuring out what to do with it after extraction.

The stainless steel wire-mesh tea ball—never the pot-metal variety with its too few holes and unpleasant taint—was my brewing device of choice for years. The main problem in using tea balls comes with large-leaf teas, which sometimes require more than one to ensure full extraction. Much flavor is lost if the leaf swells into an impenetrable mass. Teapots equipped with removable infusion baskets do not present this difficulty, and this is my preferred method today. Either way, how do you deal with the object once removed?

I like to place tea ball or infusion basket in a covered receptacle for it to drain out of sight where its utilitarian looks will not offend the eye. A stainless steel or plastic object clashes with silver and china, I think, and besides, uncontained liquid is unwise at tea gatherings. A closed container handles easily, moreover, and allows your guests to lift the lid and inhale the bouquet of the infused leaf trapped inside, if desired. This enhances the ceremony and adds to the pleasure the tea provides. Smelling the infused tea leaf should prove irresistible anyway if the tea is of any great stature. Since there's no such covered item included with tea services as yet, improvise. Tea ware is whatever you use, as the old Japanese masters knew. Only remember in choosing what to use, it must be as esthetically pleasing as it is functional. Pleasant harmony is at the heart of what every tea ceremony aims at, in every time or cultural setting.

PRACTICAL CONSIDERATIONS IN MAKING TEA

Water

Water is of paramount importance. All water is not created equal. Don't ask me why, but for making tea, some water is less than ideal, some dreadful. Chlorine and fluoride are universally added to tap water so that it harms the flavor of tea. It's no great harm if it's no great tea, but the better the tea, the more it deserves spring water, as tea lovers from the time of Lu Yu himself have rightly claimed. Such sweet-tasting spring water is not always necessary, moreover, because oftentimes even one as sodium laden as California's cheap and plentiful Calistoga Water will produce good tea—thanks to its mineral content, one supposes. Calistoga, Evian and other waters with high mineral content seem to bring out the richness and sweetness of green tea, but I think black, and other teas, take best to waters like Volvic with low mineral levels. My colleague Donald Wallace, head of the American Tea Masters Association, contends the ideal pH for any tea water is an alkaline pH of 7.9. Distilled water or that filtered by osmosis-type filters are the worst because they are stripped of mineral content.

Chapter and verse may be cited to prove that specific teas take best to certain waters. I once satisfied my curiosity in this matter by making a superb Dragon Well with water from Tiger Run Spring, the age-old prescription of Chinese connoisseurs. It may have been largely imagination, but I confess no Dragon Well has ever tasted as good to me. A less exalted example is the blend an English tea firm allegedly created specifically to go best with Manhattan water. This was in response to numerous customer complaints that their accustomed teas never tasted right when they traveled to New York. The list goes on, but that is another book.

Not to put too fine a point on it, the cheapest and simplest answer to the water question presently available seems to be the Brita brand of filter. It is a charcoal—not osmosis—type of filter device that uses papers you need to replace about once a month. Once you've acquired it from any super-market or drugstore, therefore, it costs only about ten dollars per annum to make any tap water suitable for tea-making and cooking purposes. The 1.75-liter size even fits inside refrigerators.

Temperature of Water

Water that is just coming to a boil (212 degrees Fahrenheit), or just off the boil, is ideal for black tea or most oolongs. Boiling water is much too hot for white and green teas, however. The most delicate types of green tea, like BiLuoChun, call for water that's little more than tepid. If it's too hot to pour into your palm, it's too hot to brew BiLuoChun, spring flush Longjing and their peers. You needn't be quite so fussy with most green teas, which seem at their best when brewed in water 30 to 40 degrees below boiling, or in the 170- to 185-degree-Fahrenheit range. At this tem-perature the steam from the kettle rises in lazy, curling wisps rather than in a vertical column: Let this be a sign unto you.

A word on kettles might not be out of place here. Any kettle that doesn't leak will suffice, obviously, but the inveterate tea drinker will find a special electric kettle a great convenience. The most popular brand is the Russell Hobbes kettle, but this is not ideal if you need to know more than simply whether the water's reached boiling, as per above. Because it has no lid, it's difficult judge to a nicety just how hot the water in a Hobbes kettle is. For this reason I prefer a kettle manufactured in Taiwan

and imported by Imperial Tea Court. Like the Hobbes kettle, it has a thermostat which cuts off the power once the water boils, only to kick in again once it's cooled to a certain point. Unlike the Hobbes, however, it pours with pinpoint accuracy, and, best of all, you can open the hinged lid to inspect the contents. This way you can watch the "fish eyes" form and the steam rise to judge water temperature exactly (with some practice) and easily allow the water to cool if it's too hot. In either case, if the water's come to boiling four or five times, it should be replaced with fresh. Using water with all the oxygen boiled out of it makes tea taste flat and lifeless.

Amount of Dry Leaf

"One teaspoon of tea per person and one for the pot" is not graven on stone anywhere outside the tea companies' prescriptions. You alone can decide what's "too weak." I myself tend to err on the strong side, which means I use approximately 2.5 grams of dry black tea per cup. With lighter teas—Darjeelings, say—I often use somewhat more, and somewhat less with BOPs (Broken Orange Pekoes) which quickly become astringent. I can judge such fine gradations only by using a particular Francis I dessert spoon I've employed for the purpose these many years. If you always use the same measuring spoon, you pretty well know what you're doing, and if not, not. The tricky part of measuring tea is remembering that volume and weight are not identical. There is no set guideline for just how much white, green or oolong leaf to use. The "right" amount you must discover for yourself with each tea. A rounded teaspoon of small-leaf tea will weigh more than an identically piled spoon of large-leaf tea. It takes what looks like a mighty mound of white tea, for instance, to make a single cup. Experience would seem to be the only teacher in this area.

Steeping Time

Some black teas are completely unforgiving. Fifteen seconds additional brewing time can make the difference between a perfect Darjeeling and one that's undrinkably astringent in certain cases. Large-leaf Nilgiri or Ceylon, the most forgiving of teas, can steep a minute or two longer than ideal without appreciable harm. Most others seem to lie between these extremes. The most important variable is the size of the leaf: The larger the leaf, the longer you must steep it; the smaller the leaf, the more surface it exposes to the water and the quicker the goodness is drawn out of it. Experiments with this in mind will show you the optimum brewing time for the teas you use. If you take your tea making seriously, sooner or later you will want to acquire a timer for the purpose.

Green teas by the pot should be decanted after a minute or two at most and will yield further infusions. CTC (cut-tear-curl) black teas can sometimes steep as little as a minute. As a general rule, no black tea of orthodox manufacture should steep less than three minutes. The ideal time for most Darjeelings is somewhere between three and four minutes, depending on the individual tea. Three to four minutes is ideal for most broken-leaf teas, although many a small-leaf Ceylon is best at five minutes. Ceylon OPs and other large-leaf teas—Formosa oolong, for instance—are at their best after seven minutes' steeping. Earl Grey and Lapsang Souchong should be treated like black teas, but other scented teas may vary from under three minutes upward according to taste. The shorter the steeping time, the more aroma.

How to Decaffeinate Tea

Caffeine is highly soluble and is one of the first constituents of the tea leaf to be extracted in brewing. Approximately 80 percent of the tea's caffeine content is released within the first thirty seconds of steeping. You can enjoy virtually caffeine-free tea with small sacrifice of flavor, therefore, by discarding the water after the first thirty seconds' steeping and adding fresh boiling water to the now-decaffeinated leaf. Remember, too, that tea has constituents which act to soothe and relax the body. These polyphenols begin to dissolve only in the third minute of steeping and will be almost completely extracted after five minutes. This is the secret of bedtime tea some swear by as an aid to sleep.

Food With Tea

I'll keep this short in the belief we learn to please ourselves in this department. Perhaps the most useful things I've discovered are that chocolate seems to fight tea and win in every case, and that butter-based biscuits (try saying that fast!) detract from green tea's flavor. This accounts for the kinds of cakes and other nibbles popular with tea in Asia but not the West. As you might expect, the Japanese have a centuries-old cuisine called *kaiseki* which developed specially to accompany tea, ceremonial or not. If Westerners have developed any teatime accompaniment, it must surely be the butter-based biscuit available wherever English (at least) is spoken—except in the United States. A Nabisco product called Royal Lunch comes close to my ideal of this type of hardtack, but it's inexplicably hard to find. I'm hardly the best guide in these matters, since I eat almost anything—except chocolate when tea's exceptional.

A GREEN TEA CEREMONY: THE GUYWAN METHOD

*G*uywan is Mandarin for "covered cup." It consists of saucer, bowl and lid which function together. This ingenious invention has been in use in China since the earliest days of the Ming dynasty—circa 1350—as the simplest, most satisfying way of enjoying loose-leaf tea. It is decidedly the best way to get the most enjoyment from green teas, for which it was originally developed, but also lends itself to making other teas. Let me say at the outset that it takes a lot longer to read about than it takes to learn how to do it.

Enough tea for a single cup is heaped in the bottom of the cup, where it may be seen to best advantage against the whiteness of the porcelain. (The appearance of the tea leaf before, during and after steeping is highly important to the Chinese.) With black tea, oolong or Pu-Er, you begin by "rinsing the leaves," as if they had dust on them just as, in ancient days, they probably did. The first water you pour on—well under half the *guywan*—is immediately drained off. This requires tilting the lid and using it to hold back the leaf while you pour. In handling, the cup is never removed from the saucer. You now bring the *guywan* to your nose and uncover it, breathing in the freshly released aroma of the leaf. Only now that you have inhaled its perfume is water poured on again, to steep.

With white or green teas you omit "rinsing the leaves" and steep the tea without replacing the lid. Water is not poured directly onto the tea, but on one side of the *guywan*, producing a swirl in the cup. The leaves float before your eyes and then become saturated and sink to form a floating forest in the bottom of your cup. You should unhurriedly watch this ballet of the leaf as its dissolving juices color the water, until, after a minute or so, you deem it time for a first exploratory sip, sometimes without waiting for all the leaf to sink.

Handling the *guywan* is easier to demonstrate than to describe. If right-handed, place the saucer holding the cup in the palm of your right hand, steadying the cup with thumb resting on the rim. Use the lid as a paddle (turn it on its side and paddle like an oar) to stir the liquid away from you. This roils the leaf at the cup's bottom and circulates the tea. To take a sip, use your left hand to hold the lid by its knob at a slight tilt away from your lips to serve as a sort of filter holding back the leaves. Hold the lid at this slight angle while lifting the *guywan* to your mouth with your right hand under the saucer. All this is less complicated than it sounds—you quickly get the hang of it and before long your gestures develop elegance and grace.

Water is added before you drain the cup to keep the tea a-brewing out more and more of the goodness of the leaf. Only when water is added the third time is it poured directly into the middle of the infused leaf, which serves not to swirl but to invert the mass. Any China tea yields multiple infusions, and one discovers what subtly different tastes emerge from a second, third and fourth infusion compared to the first. This process may be repeated as long as the leaf yields flavor.

It is important to use water between 170 and 185 degrees Fahrenheit in brewing white and green teas—the more delicate the tea, the lower the temperature. Water that's too hot gives the liquor a yellowish tinge, a sure sign the leaf's nectar has been cooked instead of extracted. The cooler the water, in turn, the longer the leaf may be steeped. A minute, more or less, is about right for green teas of great subtlety, allowing a little longer for each successive infusion. These are the least forgiving of all teas to make to perfection. In making such for guests, use a single *guywan* which can be drained at the proper instant into a small pitcher, from which you fill thimble cups. With less exalted green teas, each person can drink from his own *guywan*, and serving guests is just a matter of replenishing each *guywan* with hot water at the appropriate intervals.

With black, oolong or Pu-Er teas, use just-boiling water, cover the cup, and allow considerably longer steeping time. These teas are not only less beautiful to watch infuse, they also taste better hotter. Black tea should always be decanted to prevent oversteeping or, if using an infusion, remove it before serving the tea.

Classic *guywans* are hard to find in the United States, even in Chinatown shops selling the much commoner mug with lid and handle called a *zhong*. They may be bought from Ten Ren shops or by mail order from Imperial Tea Court or my own catalog, which I established chiefly to fill the need for hard-to-find tea wares. Once acquired, however, the *guywan* is, like paper and printing and china itself, another of those Chinese inventions which one can't imagine doing without—the simplest, most satisfying way of preparing and enjoying tea all day and night long.

THE CLASSIC OOLONG CEREMONY: THE KUNG-FU METHOD

Kung-fu means "skill and practice" or "time and trouble" or "patient effort." It refers not to the martial arts alone but to the human factor required to master any art. On account of the extra steps involved in producing black tea, the Chinese called them kung-fu teas, which English corrupted to "Congou," the name by which China black tea is still known by tea blenders.

Like the teapot itself, first produced in Yi-xing potteries circa 1492, China's kung-fu tea ritual dates from the Ming dynasty and is at least five thousand years old. Oolong devotees in south China have perfected this elegant way to brew unbelievably wonderful tea. The art, besides being a delight in itself, is also a good deal cheaper than other forms of therapy. With a little practice using Yi-xing ware to brew tea, your kung-fu will be a wonder to your friends and an abiding pleasure for yourself. And your tea will be superb. The accoutrements needed can be obtained from the same sources that sell *guywans*. To start, at least, there's no need for Yi-xing pots made by famous masters, which can cost thousands.

Seated at a table, you arrange your utensils so that the kettle is to your right (if right-handed) and implements with tea towel to your left. On the drainer in front of you, place the tea boat, a small pitcher (if desired) and the thimble cups (the saucers should be positioned in front of each guest). The teapot sits in the boat. The first order of business is to clean and warm these utensils.

Using boiling water, fill the teapot. Pour the water off into thimble cups and then empty these into the pitcher. The bamboo tweezers may be used to empty thimbles, though fingers work too if you're careful.

Allow your guests to inspect the dry leaf you have selected before filling the pot half to two-thirds full of it. For this step, you may wish to pour the leaf onto a small saucer and use the bent bamboo stick to scrape it gently into the teapot. Sometimes I use paper instead and make a funnel through which the tea may be easily poured into the teapot's opening. Either way, take your time. Make your gestures slow and grace-ful and the ritual becomes one of intimacy and tranquillity.

"Rinse the leaves" by filling the pot with boiling water, which is immediately poured off into the drainer (or a waste receptacle if you don't use a drainer). Use both hands to pass the open pot, resting on the tea towel, for everyone to enjoy the full aroma of the tea.

Now fill the teapot, making sure to pour the water over all the leaf, not just in the middle. Replace the lid at once and pour more scalding water over the outside of the pot itself to collect in the tea boat and maintain maximum heat for brewing. Because of the monster amount of tea used, brewing requires seconds, not minutes. After five or six slow breaths, the tea is ready to decant. Use both hands to hold the pot by the handle and lid and, using a circular motion, scrape the bottom of the pot a time or two around the rim of the tea boat. This eliminates the water running off the pot while swirling the tea inside it. Be patient with yourself: Don't worry about "doing it wrong." It all becomes second nature soon enough.

Decant into the pitcher and fill cups. If you prefer pouring directly into the cups, make sure they're grouped in a squadron or line, lip-to-lip. The pouring can be con-tinuous as each thimble cup is filled halfway and then topped up in reverse order, to assure uniform strength.

Thimble cups may be placed on the saucer before each guest, or they may pick them up from the drainer. When served, guests often tap the table lightly beside the cup with a finger or two to say "Thank you." Chinese hosts gesture with the hands, palm up, to say "Please taste." Polite words are unnecessary.

Tea brewed kung-fu-style will be quite concentrated, with an intensity of aroma and flavor otherwise unobtainable. Sip it like a liqueur. The aftertaste of a fine oolong may linger up to half an hour afterward.

Pot after pot may be brewed in this way with slightly longer steeping time allowed for each. Any fine oolong should yield five or six brews before the flavor begins to wane appreciably, but each brewing brings out subtly altered nuances to enjoy. The Chinese say the first is most fragrant, the second strongest and the third the sweetest brew.

The tea towel is used throughout to wipe up any drops that go astray. Any undrunk tea is poured into the drainer before a fresh infusion is made and at the end of the session. Then the leaf is dislodged from the pot with the curved bamboo and the cups are rinsed. Rinse but never wash the pot. The porous earthenware absorbs flavor each time it's used. Tea can actually be made in old, frequently used pots just by adding boiling water. For this reason, a Yi-xing pot should be dedicated to use with a single kind of tea. If you make Jasmine or Pu-Er teas kung-fu-style, do not use your oolong pot!

A new earthenware pot must be broken in before it is used. If intended for oolong, for instance, it should be boiled in a saucepan with oolong tea leaves and allowed to soak in it five to six hours to remove the odor of the clay.

THE JAPANESE TEA CEREMONY: CHANOYU

Whereas the point of Chinese tea ceremonies is the tea, what matters most to the Japanese is the ceremony. The famous Japanese tea ceremony is without doubt the most ritualized way of drinking tea practiced anywhere. Some devotees dedicate their lives to *chanoyu*, which translates as "hot water for tea," and volumes have been written on the subject. It is obviously not the same thing as merely drinking tea, but what it is, exactly, is harder to define.

The basic procedures for this tea ceremony were laid down by a Buddhist practitioner named Sen-no Rikyu (1522–1591), who modified and refined what was already an ancient tradition with roots in Song dynasty China (960–1279). The best Song teas were manufactured in cake form and were prepared by powdering the leaf, which was not steeped but added to hot water and whipped with a bamboo whisk. Only one cup at a time could be prepared in this way, obviously, and one drank this liquid with the leaf suspended in it, powder and all. Whipped tea was restricted to the Song nobility and their favored elite among the Buddhist monks. This ruling class was dispossessed, if not exterminated, as the Mongols under Kublai Khan (1215–1294) completed the conquest of China, and their tea tradition died with them. Only in Japan, where it had taken root and the Mongols did not penetrate, has whipped tea been preserved.

The tea ceremony Rikyu codified and taught thus had centuries of aristocratic precedents. It had become a symbol of new wealth and culture to Japanese warlords and merchants who vied to acquire prized antique tea wares, paintings and artifacts associated with tea. Knowing how to use and display such treasures and mastering the etiquette involved in making and serving tea conferred enormous social prestige, and the philosophy known as the Way of Tea was considered a path to spiritual attainment closely associated with Zen, the samurais' preferred form of Buddhism. Rikyu learned the art from a disciple of an earlier master, Shuko, who maintained, "It is not an amusement, nor a technique either, but an enjoyment of enlightened satisfaction."

The full ceremony involves a meal and two servings of tea and takes almost half

a day. It is usually practiced in a shortened form, bequeathed by Rikyu, which takes about forty-five minutes. Guests enter the tea room and admire the host's hanging scroll, flower arrangement, brazier and tea utensils, then, in a row, seat themselves on their knees. The host enters the room and sets a container of sweets before the guests, then departs and returns carrying the tea bowl and additional tea implements. He seats himself opposite the guests and proceeds to prepare and serve a bitter, frothy tea— Matcha—of a vivid green color. Each guest eats a sweet while observing the preparations.

Each mimelike gesture, from the host's folding of a silk cloth, to pouring the water and whisking the tea, to the guests' acceptance of the bowl, admiring it before sipping and showing appreciation for other tea utensils, is designed to be simple, natural and beautiful. At the same time, this fastidious adherence to form leaves nothing to choice. The placement of the tea bowl must correspond to a certain row of stitching in the tatami mat. When entering the room, guests must cross the threshold with the right foot, and when leaving, with the left. It requires years of untiring discipline of body and mind, obviously, to become an accomplished *chajin*, or "tea person."

"It puts you in a calm, quiet place. You have to focus on what you're doing so the rest of the world disappears. Sometimes I'll walk out of the tea room and my whole day will be changed," says Linda Morse, a San Francisco jewelry appraiser who has studied tea for two years. More and more Americans have been drawn to study *chanoyu* either with private teachers or at the different branches of the Urasenke Foundation, one of the largest Japanese tea schools. In San Francisco there is a waiting list for its ten-session introductory course. The Way of Tea leads to the peace and poetry of life which we all seek, and students of the Way eventually realize its formalities and rules are not meant as obstacles, nor as an end in themselves, but act like a finger pointing at the moon.

The life of Rikyu is inseparable from his teachings, and his death by *seppuku*, or ritual suicide, is the central event in the history of *chanoyu*. It is a story Hiroshi Teshigahara, director of the famous *Woman in the Dunes*, devoted years to filming, and the resulting movie, *Rikyu*, probably captures the man and his work better than any book. Rikyu's teaching may be summarized in the untranslatable words *wabi-sabi*, which mean much more than "simple and natural." It is an attitude not only toward beauty but toward Seeing itself, and life.

Once the shogun learned that Rikyu grew wonderful morning-glories and everybody marveled at his garden in bloom. Having sent word to Rikyu of his intention to pay a visit, the shogun duly arrived but found not a single morning-glory to be seen. Only once he was inside the tea room did he behold in the alcove a single morning-glory of surpassing beauty. Earlier that morning Rikyu had torn up all the others, preserving just this one exquisite flower.

Another time Rikyu called on a humble friend whom he found busy working in his field. They went home together and entered the house. There, standing in the alcove, to greet Rikyu, was the hoe his friend had just been using in the field, still wet and dirty. Setting it up in such a place of honor showed its importance to its owner, and Rikyu found such taste admirable. Prettiness has no place in the wabi-sabi ideal of beauty.

Why do we long for beauty? Rikyu would reply that the world of beauty is our home and that we are born with a love for home. But home, he might add, is the realm of Non-duality: Everything that has been divided longs to be reunited; everything has been divided in order to long to be one again. Regarding a beautiful object, then, is like looking at one's own native home, the original nature of Man himself. To acquire a thing of beauty is really buying oneself, and to look at a beautiful object is to see in it one's completed, primordial self. The Japanese cult of the tea ceremony aims beyond beauty, whether of objects or of comportment, at glimpses of the Ultimate.

Traditional Tea Utensils

CHINESE

Drainer—A round porcelain or metal tray on which a teapot is placed. The drainer has holes on the top for wastes, when the top is removed, the dregs of the teas and the excess water are there to be thrown away after the guests have left.

Glasses—Usually highball-style glasses, sometimes used for a special green tea that rises and falls while infusing in a tall glass. Wineglasses may also be used for some specialized green teas which are hand-tied to form flowers or balls and unfurl into shapes two or three times their size when fully brewed.

Guywan—The classic, traditional vessel for drinking tea, Chinese-style, with matching saucer to hold the cup and a lid for paddling leaves as they unfurl.

Gongfu (Kung-fu) Implements—Usually sold as a set, they include tweezers, to hold on to hot cups; a large scoop for measuring out tea from a canister and placing it in a pot; and a long narrow scraper that is curved at one end and pointed at the other. The curved end is used to separate stems and leaves prior to infusion, and the pointed end is used to gently scrape out tea leaves which may be stuck in the teapot. All three are placed in a holder. They can be rough-hewn or quite elegantly made from light woods. Typically, Chinese eschew these implements and simply use their fingers.

Teacups—Usually half the size of English teacups and about four times as big as a thimble cup, these handleless cups are usually used for China black and sometimes oolong teas.

Thimble Cups—These cups are small, usually 1 1/4 inches in diameter, and are often available with matching saucer. They are used in the kung-fu-style tea ceremony, particularly for delicate white, yellow or green teas, although they can certainly be used for any tea one likes.

Yixing Teapot—The original, and some still say the best, teapot in the world, made of unique clay from the Yixing province in China. It is so absorbent and special that teapots used over the years are said to take on the flavor of the tea and can be used even when only water is poured into the pot. Comes in traditional reddish clay and also brown and ochre from the ores in the red clay. The teal colors are oxidized.

Zhong—Used to denote a covered cup, this word has now come to mean a mug, with or without saucer, with a lid.

JAPANESE

The Japanese tea ceremony *Chanoyu* is a precise, contrived, exquisitely choreographed tea ceremony often taking years to perfect. The utensils are simply and beautifully made, frequently heirlooms handed down from one generation to the next, and consist primarily of small tea canisters, tea bowls (or cups), iron tea kettles for heating water, water scoops, brush for foaming up the green tea plus special tea napkins used by the hostess or host. The best source for more information is your local Urasenke Center (New York, Los Angeles and San Francisco) or *Chan-o-yu*, a wonderful book by A. L. Sadler. Contemporary and traditional ceramic artists have perfected the Raku teapot, an elegant small teapot usually shown with an extra tall handle.

ENGLISH/EUROPEAN

$\mathcal{B}$**rown Betty**—the traditional brown teapot from clay native to England which has particularly good warming capabilities; usually glazed on the outside and unglazed inside, although modern ones are glazed on the inside as well. Look for the *A* mark on the bottom of the pot.

Lemon Fork—Tiny two-pronged forks used to spear lemons to drop into unsuspecting teas.

Mote Spoon—Taken from the Dutch word *mot*, meaning "dust." It is a pierced spoon with a pointed end on its handle used to stick into the spout of a teapot to scoop out wayward leaves.

Slop Bowl—A bowl for the "slop," or drips, that may piddle down from an urn or samovar, thus preventing them from spotting a cloth.

Strainer—Modern answer to the mote spoon. Shaped like an oversized spoon, it can be made of metal, porcelain or a wire mesh and is used to catch the leaves brewed loose in a teapot. Simply pour tea through strainer and, voilà, the strainer catches the wayward leaves.

Sugar Tongs—A must-have to grab hold of sugar cubes to plop in one's tea.

Tea Caddy—A canister or container of tea first introduced to England during the first half of the eighteenth century and often created of beautiful woods. Some caddies have three compartments, two for tea, and the center glass for mixing, although later on when sugar was in greater supply, many caddies used the center glass container to hold the precious sugar. Caddies have also been made of every source imaginable, from metal to glass to porcelain. "Caddy" is from the Malay word *kati*, or "one pound," referring to the original small box first imported to England which contained, in fact, 1.2 pounds of tea.

Tea Caddy Spoon—Usually shell shaped (scallop shells were the original scoops for tea), caddy spoons are often quite elaborate sterling silver affairs, but can be humble stainless, wood or silver plate.

Tea Cosy—The debate will rage into the next millennium about whether cosies help to stew the tea, decanted or not, or simply help keep it warm. At any rate, they are fabric, usually quilted, in a variety of shapes and patterns that fit over teapots and serve as a nice decoration as well as doing their perfunctory duty to keep tea hot.

Teapots for English-style tea may be silver, earthenware or porcelain, and many eighteenth-century ones still remain in use. Collectors prize them for their shapes, styles and decorations. Earthenware is well-known for its ability to keep tea hot.

Teapoy describes either the end table on which a teapot is placed during tea service, or a wooden tea caddy permanently affixed to a three-legged table.

OTHER IMPLEMENTS

Celadon Porcelain—The primary material used in Korean teapots. Imitations of this pale green porcelain are plentiful in Japan; it serves as a wonderful mirror for enjoying the colors of tea.

Glasses with handles or glasses with elaborately filigreed holders with handles are traditional in Russia.

Samovar—A cousin of the Mongolian cooking pot, a samovar usually contains a funnel inside it for hot coals to heat the water. An elongated pipe was then attached to the top of the funnel and through the roof so that the smoke of the coals would vent outside. Present-day samovars are often electrified and are a valuable addition to teas at which you entertain many people, as it keeps the water hot. A truly Russian invention. Modern stainless steel ones are best, but decorative painted ones with folk art designs are also available from Russia.

Tea and Health

❧ ❧

D r. Thomas Stuttaford, writing in the London *Times* of March 28, 1995, told his British readers: "Recent research from Japan reported in the *British Medical Journal* has analyzed the effect of green tea drinking on 1,371 men who live in Yoshimi; it found that the portents for reduction in the incidence of coronary heart disease and cardiovascular diseases in general were good." After reporting further test results suggesting green tea drinking may provide protection against cancers of the liver, colon and lungs, Dr. Stuttaford remarks, "Green tea devotees have always claimed that it is not only refreshing and a help to the digestion but also has other medicinal properties with a longer-term advantage. Science has now shown that they may be right."

Dr. Stuttaford illustrates the way modern scientific research on tea and health must be interpreted for general consumption. The countless scientific papers on the subject now available from many sources tend to have two things in common: Most show evidence of tea's benefits, and all are impenetrable to the nonspecialist reader.

 Results like these have been turning up ever since research into the potential health benefits of drinking tea began around 1970 at the Mitsui Norin Food Research Laboratories in Japan. (Green tea was chosen for study because 99 percent of all the tea consumed in Japan is green, but tests elsewhere often draw largely similar conclusions concerning black tea drinking.)

Such findings are not exactly new. The author of *Chinese Tea and Health*, a book published in 1988, reviewed over five hundred references to Chinese traditional medicine and concluded that by 200 B.C. tea had sixty-one applications for the prevention of disease and some two hundred uses as a cure for various illnesses. By 200 B.C. tea had already been used as an herbal medicine for some two thousand years in China. Returning to modern science, it is hardly surprising that Dr. Hara of Mitsui Norin now claims preliminary evidence indicates the following:

- Tea contains natural antioxidants that can help fight cancer and aid in the prevention of tumors.
- Tea can help reduce plasma total cholesterol and LDL cholesterol.
- Tea contains polyphenols that inhibit the enzymes that convert starch to glucose, thereby lowering glucose levels.
- Tea contains polyphenols that inhibit the angiotension converting enzyme that is known to cause hypertension.
- Tea has antibacterial properties that can inhibit staphylococcus and streptococcus infections.
- Tea contains theraflavins and therarubigins that can help to relieve asthmatic and respiratory inflammations.
- Tea is a natural source of fluoride, which is essential in preventing tooth decay.
- Tea helps to inhibit the growth of plaque on teeth.
- Tea contains a bioflavanoid called vitamin P which strengthens capillary blood vessels.
- Tea is a natural source of manganese, which aids the body's protein and energy metabolism.
- Tea contains theanine, a unique amino acid found nowhere else, which modifies and alleviates the pharmacological effects of the caffeine tea contains, making its ingestion easier for the body.

If you have understood the above, it is quite unnecessary for you to read any more of this chapter—unless, that is, you are curious about caffeine, the first of these topics I shall attempt to tackle.

CAFFEINE

$\mathcal{T}$he medical dosage of caffeine given to patients to offset fatigue, drowsiness and the like is 200 milligrams. Roughly speaking, one would need to drink at least four cups of black tea in one sitting to approximate the medical dosage. It would take twelve cups of green tea or six cups of oolong to provide this much caffeine.

Caffeine stimulates the nervous system, removes fatigue and sleepiness and enhances one's ability to think. It stimulates metabolism and the process of elimination and acts as a diuretic, promoting better kidney function. Stimulation of the heart and lungs brings more oxygen to the brain, increasing mental alertness and shortening reaction time. Caffeine increases the amount of work that can be performed by the muscles, without increasing blood pressure or heart rate. Thus, it acts on both mind and muscles. The body reacts to caffeine by creating stimulant chemicals called catecholamines, which relay nerve impulses to the brain. The height of this effect lasts from fifteen to forty-five minutes. After six hours, the body has eliminated half the caffeine

Caffeine is no doubt the most thoroughly studied substance people use. It is an alkaloid which occurs in over sixty different plants, few of which are related to one another. It was isolated from coffee beans in 1820. In 1837 this was shown to be identical with the alkaloid found in tea leaves and previously called theine.

Caffeine in Coffee and Tea

There is more caffeine in a pound of tea (4.5 percent) than in a pound of coffee (2.5–3.5 percent); but the pound of coffee produces about forty cups, whereas the pound of tea produces about two hundred cups, as per industry averages. The typical cup of coffee—non-espresso-type—thus contains about 125 to 185 milligrams of caffeine. *Consumer Reports* analyzed eighteen leading supermarket tea-bag brands of black tea and found an average of about 55 milligrams per cup. Because mass market tea-bag teas consist largely or exclusively of fannings and dust (finely powdered tea leaf), brewing extracts almost all the caffeine present. This is not the case with larger-leaf or non-tea-bag teas, which accordingly yield smaller amounts of caffeine in the range of 45 to 50 milligrams per cup. Green tea has about one-third as much caffeine as black tea does; oolong has about two-thirds as much.

Reactions to Caffeine

There are undoubtedly caffeine-sensitive people who must avoid this stimulant, but they seem to be a relatively small proportion of the population. For the rest, tolerance varies and addiction is the rule. Consuming caffeine to excess can lead to jitteriness, sleeplessness and an increased need to urinate, but this passes without any long-term effects. There is, however, the caffeine headache, familiar to everybody who has grown addicted to immoderate intake. This can result either from excess caffeine or from not getting enough to satisfy the increased tolerance. In my own experience, I find these rather mild, as headaches go, and far from frequent. The cure seems to be returning to the Golden Mean, whatever that means in your own case.

Many people report that tea does not prevent sleep, but sometimes it does in my experience, and I am not among those who take a bedtime cup of strong black tea. It is rare, however, to suffer sleeplessness as a result of any amount of green or oolong consumed in an evening.

At all events, the effects of caffeine from tea as opposed to coffee are rather hard to compare. The caffeine in coffee takes effect immediately, while with tea there is a delay of ten to fifteen minutes. "Coffee nerves" with accompanying anxiety states and the rest are unknown to tea drinkers, who must drink quantities indeed to experience even mild jitters. With tea, the lift the caffeine provides is not followed by a letdown or accompanied by the unpleasant gastric sensations which can result from drinking coffee. Tea can actually produce more of a soothing, calming effect than stimulation, or—more frequently—produces both together.

How to Decaffeinate Tea

The caffeine content is extracted in the first two minutes after boiling water is poured onto tea leaves, although a residual amount remains in the leaf. In fact, 80 percent of the caffeine is extracted in the first thirty seconds. This means anybody watching caffeine intake can easily decaffeinate any tea he or she likes by the simple expedient of throwing away the water after thirty seconds and starting to steep the leaves all over again. Comparatively very little of the flavor will be sacrificed, since these constituents are slower to dissolve. The resulting cup will contain the negligible amount of 10 milligrams or less caffeine if an orthodox black tea is used (less if an oolong is used and even less than that if you use a green tea.)

This rather neat trick enables the caffeine-sensitive to enjoy the same fine and great teas the rest of us do. It's a useful technique to remember on those occasions when one wants more tea but no more caffeine.

Tea begins to release its tannins only in the third minute of steeping. Tannins, polyphenols that is, which are not present in coffee's chemical makeup, serve to cancel or mollify the effects of caffeine. Since they dissolve from the third through fifth minute of steeping, black tea brewed five minutes or more will be found more relaxing and calming than it is stimulating.

The Caffeine Controversies

Except for the caffeine-sensitive minority, caffeine turns out to be not-so-bad for you. Most users grow addicted but find withdrawal relatively painless. Innumerable studies have been made, nearly all using coffee but involving tea by implication. Certain early studies linked caffeine to pancreatic cancer and heart disease, but further research has not borne this out. Surveying all such questions raised, the *University of California at Berkeley Wellness Letter* concluded in 1988 that tea or coffee drunk in moderation has no harmful effect whatever. Moderation was defined as 200 to 250 milligrams daily— say two cups of coffee or four or five cups of black tea. Pregnant women and nursing mothers were urged not to exceed moderation, however, because a fetus or infant cannot eliminate caffeine efficiently.

A research study of 45,589 coffee-drinking men aged forty to seventy years, directed by the Harvard School of Medicine, found that these coffee drinkers were no more susceptible to strokes or heart attacks than anybody else. Women were not included in the sample, however. More recent studies have found caffeine innocent in other connections and have begun to look into its positive contributions to health. To cite my favorite example, the caffeine in tea has proved invaluable in treating gout. It seems to have cured mine. Thus, it now appears the concerns raised about caffeine over the years are groundless, not to say silly, just as many suspected all along.

TEA CHEMISTRY

By the end of the nineteenth century the chemical constituents of the tea leaf had been more or less determined, though even today our understanding remains incomplete. Black tea contains about 55 percent insoluble and 45 percent soluble matter. Thus, 55 percent of the tea leaf is discarded as waste, but to this is added about 12 percent of the soluble matter which fails to be extracted in typical brewing of three to five minutes. Insoluble matter includes the leaf fiber, some proteins and a certain amount of caffeine and nitrogen.

Of the 33 percent of black tea ingredients which dissolve during a typical infusion, about 50 percent are tea tannins and 15 percent consist of amino acids. The rest consists of almost equal amounts of caffeine, minerals, sugars, pectins and organic acids. Tea contains appreciable amounts of fluoride and of vitamins E and K. It also contains yellow and red pigments and essential oils. One cup of unadulterated black tea has four calories.

Tannins

Besides caffeine, there are two other principal chemical ingredients in tea: essential oils and tannins, which are more correctly designated as polyphenols. The essential oils are also known as aromatics, because they provide tea's perfume, or as volatiles, because they evaporate totally in strong heat or over an extended time. It is the evaporation of volatiles which renders tea stale. Whether formed during the growth of the leaf or during manufacture, these oils are reduced by the full fermentation black tea undergoes. This is why black tea has less aroma than green.

Just as the term "fermentation" as applied to tea making really means oxidation, since no alcohol is formed, it is likewise a time-honored misnomer to speak of "tannins" in tea. They received this name long before modern methods of chemical analysis revealed that they are not tannins at all. Tannins come from many sources. Some possess the property of hardening animal tissues, turning hide into leather; others are mildly astringent and employed in products like face lotion. Tannic acid and other commercial tannins are chemically quite different from tea tannin, which has no tanning effect on the stomach lining or elsewhere.

The chemically correct name for tea tannins is "polyphenols"; there are about thirty altogether. Polyphenols account for tea's pungency, the astringent puckery feeling it gives the mouth. This stimulates the salivary glands, which is why tea is a thirst quencher. Green tea is more astringent than black or oolong because it does not undergo the fermentation which oxidizes one-third to one-half of the polyphenols into more complicated products.

The unoxidized polyphenols—colorless, astringent, and bitter to the taste—are responsible for the character of green tea. Black tea's color and flavor are due to the polyphenols oxidized during fermentation. The less oxidized, semifermented oolong has greater pungency and lighter color than black teas. The polyphenols are chemically the most interesting component in tea's makeup and seem to do the most good for human health.

TEA TANNIN AND MILK

The oxidized polyphenols in tea bind to milk's casein. This renders the tea less harsh to the taste and to the stomach and more readily assimilable into the system. About one teaspoon of milk to a five-ounce cup is sufficient for this purpose; more than that begins to bind the remaining unoxidized polyphenols responsible for the needed pungency. Milk does not cut down on the beneficial effects of these tannins on the body, however.

It has also been established that artificial sweeteners are safe with tea and create no chemical reactions. A University of Wisconsin study shows that the addition of lemon juice increases the solubility of tea's iron and calcium content by about 25 percent. However, milk and lemon juice should never be used together, as the lemon juice will curdle the milk and render the tea undrinkable.

TEA AND MENTAL HEALTH

Accounts of tea's effect on mental activity may seem exaggerated, but tests have been carried out on groups of people doing arithmetical additions of comparable difficulty before and after drinking tea. After drinking tea, they needed about 25 percent less time to complete the series, and the number of mistakes declined by 25 percent as well.

Undoubtedly, mental health is tea's chief contribution to human well-being and happiness. As John Blofeld said in *The Chinese Art of Tea*: "This art, besides being delightful in itself, is a great deal cheaper than most other forms of therapy. I have yet to hear of regular tea people who need the help of professional analysis. To be a tea man or tea woman is to doctor one's mind. Cultivation of immediate responses to the Here and Now by means of the tea art leads gently to a more permanent awareness. Thereafter, the fragile beauties of each moment, which have hitherto been allowed to pass unnoticed, will receive our pleased attention."

TEA AND THE BODY

The Chinese say, "He who drinks tea forgets the noise and unrest of daily life." Scientists have discovered that tea contains vitamin B1, known to make people less sensitive to noise and clamor, thus once again Chinese folklore corroborates science.

Traditional Chinese medicine classifies tea as a cooling agent. That it's always drunk hot is beside the point; heating and cooling are contrasting categories of effects wrought upon the body's organs. "Assuaging" and "stimulating" have been suggested as better translations. Chewed tea leaves are applied to insect bites to relieve itching. They use a tray of tea leaves burned at dusk to drive away mosquitoes. In the West, people have long bathed in tea as an antidote to sunburn, and certain of my friends bathe in tea as a substitute for sunbathing to obtain a tan.

Green tea is a source of vitamin C, which is almost completely destroyed in the fermentation producing black tea. Vitamin C is usually destroyed by heat, like boiling water, but for some unknown reason this does not occur with green tea. The amount of the vitamin present varies greatly, depending on the growing season, the age of the leaf when plucked and how long the tea has been stored. (It will be all gone after three years.) Some 85 percent of the vitamin is released in a five-minute infusion. All the more reason not to use boiling water in making green tea. Considerably cooler temperature releases not only the vitamin but green tea's infinitely more delicate taste.

The large quantities of brick tea consumed by the nomadic tribes of Mongolia and Central Asia is almost their sole source of vitamin C, because of their extensively animal diet of meat and dairy products, yet they do not suffer from scurvy or other diseases which can result from lack of vitamin C.

Tea Versus Cholesterol

In the 1960s researchers noticed arteriosclerosis is quite rare in China and that this was related to lower cholesterol levels. They also found that tea drunk during or after a greasy meal prevents an increase in the serum lipid or blood fat content. Studies show all kinds of tea reduce cholesterol, though Pu-Er and oolong seems to get the best results. Other research shows that tea constituents act to strengthen the walls of blood vessels, and Russia even markets a therapeutic concentrate extracted from green tea especially for this purpose. In *All the Tea in China*, Kit Chow documents in some detail the growing body of research which suggest that tea works against heart attacks, stroke and thrombosis.

Considerable study has been devoted to an ancient type of Yunnan tea called Pu-

Er Tuocha, following a Chinese report in the 1970s on its effects in reducing blood fats. Investigations at St. Antoine Hospital in Paris concluded that Pu-Er did help reduce body weight and blood triglycerides and cholesterol, results that were disputed by some and later confirmed by others. Researchers in Paris demonstrated that three cups of Pu-Er a day for a month brought lipids down 25 percent in twenty hyperlipidemia patients, while those on other teas showed no change. Chinese doctors and many others now prefer Pu-Er to the commonly used medicine clofibrate and say it has no side effects.

Following these findings on the effect of tea on fats in the bloodstream, Chinese claims that tea also helps reduce fat in the tissues deserve serious consideration. Chinese material cites numerous examples of weight loss by people drinking two or three cups of oolong per day, and similar claims for Pu-Er have been corroborated by Japanese research. The widely sold Chinese "Slimming Tea" is advertised to take off up to fifteen pounds, if drunk for three months.

Tea Versus Tooth Decay

Many dentists recommend tea drinking. Fluoride, of which the human body requires one to three milligrams a day, may be supplied by several cups of strong tea. (Green has twice as much as black.) Fluoride strengthens bones, warding off osteoporosis and tooth enamel, thus resisting decay. A professor at UCLA's School of Dentistry, Lawrence E. Wolinsky, has noted an exceptionally low rate of dental problems among people who drink a lot of tea. He finds tea polyphenols bind themselves to mouth bacteria before the latter can form plaque. Two other U.S. universities have found that tea drinking "significantly inhibited" the growth of mouth bacteria. In China, Xia Baltu, a toothpaste for children containing 2 percent tea, has been found superior to others in prevention of cavities.

Tea Versus Bacterial Infections

"The antibacterial effects of tea have been well-documented in Chinese scientific literature," Dr. Albert Y. Leung writes in *Chinese Herbal Remedies*. "Green teas have stronger effects than black teas. They are effective against many types of bacteria, including those that cause dysentery, diphtheria and cholera . . . particularly in treating bacillary dysentery, amoebic dysentery, acute gastroenteritis (inflammation of stomach and intestine) and enteritis."

Further research was inspired by an incident in a restaurant in Taiwan in 1980. An entire table of diners got sick from contaminated shrimp except for one man. Professor E. Ryu of National Taiwan University investigated why and concluded it was because he was a heavy tea drinker. In laboratory tests, he added tea to cultures of different bacteria and found that it kept them all, salmonella, cholera, staphylococcus and even streptococcus included, from developing. Black, green and oolong had the same effect. Tea drinking, Ryu concluded, "is a great contribution to the prevention of a variety of contagious diseases."

It has long been maintained that the growth of China's population has been aided from ancient times by the use of tea, which was relatively germ-free compared to unboiled water. It is obvious from the foregoing that even cold tea possesses antibacterial properties. This accounts for the Chinese practice of washing cuts in tea if there is nothing more medicinal on hand. They also believe washing the face with tea helps prevent breaking out and employ it as a cure for athlete's foot. Very strong tea is used for frequent foot baths over a period of several weeks. Dried used leaves are put in the socks to prevent any recurrence.

Tea Versus Cancer

Considerable research has been done on the role of tea in preventing cancer. The number one cause of death in Japan is stomach cancer, but the lowest rate of occurrence is found in Shizuoka prefecture along the coast south of Tokyo. Shizuoka is Japan's premier tea-producing district, of course, and its inhabitants consume green tea in large quantities. Professor I. Oguni did a twelve-year study based on government demographic figures and confirmed that people in low mortality areas drank tea strong and often, in contrast to those in high mortality areas, who did not. His findings are similar to those reported from a survey of China's Szechuan province in 1986 and another survey in 1986–1989 of Jiangsu province. Tea-drinking areas were also shown to have a lower incidence of liver cancer.

The often high selenium content of tea forms a natural barrier in the body against cancer. A Chinese researcher, Dr. Han Chi, has discovered that tea completely blocks the synthesis of nitrosamines, which can cause cancer in the body. Japanese scientists found that green tea inhibits the action of a synthetic carcinogen called MNNG and also of aflatoxin, a powerful carcinogen produced by mold in stored crops such as peanuts or grain.

Tea also seems to help prevent cancer by preventing cell mutation. The antioxidation action of the polyphenols in green tea have been found to inhibit mutation of DNA in healthy cells. In rats injected with a cancer-causing substance and fed green tea, no cancer developed, unlike the control group without tea. An antioxidant made from green tea and applied to the skin significantly inhibited the growth of induced skin cancer in mice. Numerous papers of this sort have been presented at international scientific symposia on tea in China, France, Germany and elsewhere.

Tea and Immunity

Tea's polyphenols have been demonstrated to increase the white blood cells which serve as "soldiers" to fight infection. In Russia, green tea is credited with normalizing thyroid hyperfunction, affording protection against developing leukemia after exposure to radiation. In China, tea extract is one of the main ingredients in a medicine widely and successfully used to offset the reduction in white blood cells which accompanies radiation therapy. The Russians say tea helps the body excrete strontium 90 before it settles in the bones, while according to the Chinese it can help even after the isotope has lodged there. A blend of black tea and *viola inconspicua* achieved a 90 percent survival rate among animals the Chinese had subjected to intense radiation. It is now certain that tea exhibits strong antimutagenic and anticarcinogenic effects in a variety of ways.

Tea Versus Aging

Albeit indirectly, tea clearly promotes longevity by performing its various curative and preventive functions. From time immemorial, the Chinese have also considered tea a vital ingredient in the elixirs of immortality (which inadvertently poisoned more than one emperor) Taoist sages were so fond of, and have held it as common knowledge that tea drinking helps one live to a ripe old age. Now modern researchers at the Fujian Institute of Traditional Medicine tell us that a 1 percent solution of Jasmine tea extended the life of fruit flies to 40.5 days, more than double that of the control group, which had plain water and lived just 16.5 days. In other tests, oolong tea doubled the life span. What compounds in tea could have this effect on insects they could not say.

The Last Word on Tea and Health

Dr. Nicholas Dirx, a renowned Dutch physician, observed the first generation of Europeans accustomed to tea drinking. In 1641, thirty-three years after tea's first appearance in Holland, Dr. Dirx wrote in his *Observations Medicae*, "Nothing is comparable to this plant. Those who use it are for that reason alone exempt from maladies and reach an extreme old age. Not only does it procure great vigor for their bodies, but it preserves them from gravels and gallstones, headaches, colds, opthalmia, catarrh, asthma, sluggishness of the stomach and intestinal troubles. It has the additional merit of preventing sleep and facilitating vigils, which makes it a great help to people desiring to spend their nights writing or meditating."

Dr. Dirx's medical colleagues alive today would be obliged to concur, by and large, in his professional opinion, based on the evidence of modern science. But how many of them would be capable of such close and penetrating observation of the long-term effects of a new plant decoction? The contemporary Indian writer Arup Kumar Dutra, who wrote *Cha Garam! The Tea Story*, has well expressed the present state of our knowledge of tea's benefits. "The traditional concept of tea as a medicinal beverage has therefore been irrefutably established by modern scientific research, although work on the various aspects is not yet complete. Tea can assist in reducing weight, lowering plasma cholesterol, enriching blood, increasing appetite and promoting digestion, preventing coronary heart diseases, resisting cancer, reducing hypertension, etc. The ancient Taoists in China were not far off the mark when they eulogized tea as a divine remedy for a variety of ailments. Tea indeed is a health-giving, life-prolonging beverage—or in Taoist terms, "the elixir of immortality!"

Part 3

Exceptional Tearooms
of the United States

❦ ❧

The tearoom is having an enormously popular resurgence everywhere in the United States, from the smallest farm towns, where "tearoom" is often a euphemism for a ladies' luncheon place, to the most cosmopolitan of cities, where you can find tea at luxurious hotels and funky out-of-the way eateries. More than five hundred places serve some form of afternoon tea or Oriental or Indian tea (chai) or simply offer teas to sip without a full-service tea menu. Rather than list them all here, we have selected those we feel have either stood the test of time, offer unique or unusual tea experiences, or signal what tea drinking could be like in the future.

The list includes hotels and restaurants that offer afternoon tea, ubiquitous stand-alone tearooms, and retail shops, usually selling antiques or gift items, that also serve tea. Nearly 98 percent of these places offer European or British-style tea service which includes cream tea (crumpets or scones, pastries plus tea), afternoon tea (scones, sandwiches, tea breads, candies or petit fours and other desserts plus tea) and, rarely but increasingly, a high-tea menu which usually includes heartier sandwiches, sometimes scones or crumpets but always savories, i.e., sausage rolls, Cornish pasties, potted shrimp, selected cheeses and a bracing cup of tea.

As more and more retailers learn about fine teas, they are providing an appropriate environment for sipping exceptional teas like Ti Kuan Yin Oolong, or a fresh Longjing. Fine teas require little in the way of food to be enjoyed. It is, however, both delicious and fun to experiment in matching foods with teas just as you would match them with wines. This is still in the experimental stage and, as with all great beverages and foods, your palate is certainly the best, and final, judge.

Most of the places listed below offer good teas and some serve great teas, but generally these are places of respite where tea has a supporting role to the charm or luxury of a setting where you can set aside your cares for a while. To get the best teas, exercise your rights as a consumer and demand them!

These places are listed alphabetically by city. Times and prices change so rapidly, we suggest you call ahead for reservations, particularly during any holiday or tourist season.

TEA PLACES: A SELECTED LIST

Atlanta

The Ritz-Carlton Atlanta, 181 Peachtree St., N.E., (404) 659-0400. Served daily in the lobby lounge, with twelve selections of teas and Ritz-Carlton-style delicate menu favorites like Chelsea buns and open-faced hors-d'oeuvres-style sandwiches.

Boston

The Copley Plaza, a Wyndham Hotel, 138 St. James Ave. in Back Bay, overlooking Copley Place, (617) 267-5300. Tea Court, part of this elegant 1912 hotel, offers tea daily from an à la carte menu and classic English blends.

Charleston, South Carolina

The Charleston Place Hotel, 130 Market St., (803) 722-4900. An experienced tea leaf reader is just part of the fun of tea staged in the lobby lounge of this delightful Southern institution, which is open for afternoon tea Monday through Saturday with two set menus. Perfect place for parties.

Chicago

The Drake Hotel, 140 East Walton Place (312) 787-2200. The exquisite Palm Court is the perfect place to dine on afternoon tea daily at this venerable institution, one of the last bastions of elegance in this city.

Park Hyatt, 800 N. Michigan Ave. (312) 280-2222. While they only serve afternoon tea on Sundays, it is definitely an entertainment fit for your most important occasions from showers to birthdays to special anniversaries.

The Ritz-Carlton Chicago (a Four Seasons Hotel), 160 E. Pearson St., (312) 266-1000. Luxurious tea dining in the skylit, carpeted Greenhouse on the lobby level with soothing sounds of a fountain nearby. Choice of eleven teas to pair with one of three menus. Served daily.

Chicago Area

Seasons of Long Grove, 314 Old McHenry Rd., Long Grove, Ill., (708) 634-9150. A creative spin makes the tea foods here very special; open daily except Sunday. Major shopping in this nineteenth-century vintage town.

Dallas

The Adolphus Hotel, 1321 Commerce St., (214) 742-8200. The premier classic hotel of this Texas city draws visitors from around the world for its old-fashioned service and timeless style. Enjoy tea Monday through Friday in the lobby outside the Bistro Restaurant.

Lady Primrose's Shopping the English Countryside in the Hotel Crescent Court, 500 Crescent Court, (214) 871-8333. Full-set tea is served in the store's Thatched Cottage

Pantry Monday through Saturday, but be forewarned, the delectables are delicious and the accessories and antiques that surround you are habit-forming. Bring credit cards.

Denver

Brown Palace Hotel, 321 Seventeenth St., (303) 297-3111. Visitors to this mile-high city would be amiss if they didn't stop by this gold-rush-era opulent hotel, especially for tea Monday through Saturday in the lobby, where a harpist soothes you and the fine teas and foods comfort you.

Houston

The Ritz-Carlton Hotel Houston, 1919 Briar Oaks Lane, (713) 840-7600. In a Special Tea Lounge set aside for this special treat, you can enjoy tea daily with hospitality that is uniquely Texan and Ritz-Carlton.

Jacksonville, Oregon

Bri-tish Fare, Ltd., 235 E. California St., (503) 899-7777. Set in an historic 1868 home, this charming tearoom offers value and wit with their teas, served daily with Lyons Assam Quick Brew for a decided English touch. Also provides sympathy for fifty cents; what a bargain!

Los Angeles and Beverly Hills

The Beverly Hills Hotel, 9641 Sunset Blvd., Beverly Hills, (310) 276-2251. After several years of remodeling, this venerable hotel to the stars is bringing back its traditional afternoon tea. Stop by the tea lounge in the lobby and see what wonders they have done to this classic beauty. (P.S.: The food's great.)

Los Angeles Biltmore Hotel, 506 S. Grand Ave., Los Angeles, (213) 624-1011. The grand baroque, black wrought-iron staircase is just one of the touches of elegance surrounding the Rendezvous Court, where two full afternoon menus are served daily.

A great people-watching place and an ideal spot for a light meal before the theater or just to avoid the five-o'clock traffic rush.

Chado, 8422 1/2 W. Third St., Los Angeles, (213) 655-2056. This is the tea shop that revolutionized tea drinking in Los Angeles. Tiny, serene, elegant, with fine food and an excellent choice of teas from around the world. Good spot for a great cup. Open daily.

Four Seasons Hotel, 300 S. Doheny Drive, Los Angeles, (310) 273-2222. Full afternoon tea served weekdays in the cafe and in the Windows Lounge on Saturdays. Great food and relaxed atmosphere.

Hotel Bel Air, 701 Stone Canyon Rd., Los Angeles, (310) 472-1211. The Dining Room, with its quiet atmosphere, soft lighting, fireplace and comfortable upholstered chairs, is the perfect place to rendezvous or close a deal. Tea served weekdays.

Wyndham Checkers Hotel, 535 S. Grand Ave., Los Angeles, (213) 624-0000. The elegant lobby or the library are venues for afternoon tea served daily with your choice of twelve teas.

Pacific Dining Car, 1310 W. Sixth St., Los Angeles, (213) 483-6000, and 2700 Wilshire Blvd., Santa Monica, (310) 453-4000. This classic American-style restaurant is famous for its steaks and gargantuan breakfasts, but tea is always serenely presented and a great comfort in its predictability.

The Peninsula Beverly Hills, 9882 Little Santa Monica Blvd., Beverly Hills, (310) 273-4888. Three levels of tea served daily from three to six P.M. in the Living Room, a sun-splashed yellow and beige area of silk sofas and gracious table setting areas.

The Regent Beverly Wilshire Hotel, 9500 Wilshire Blvd., Beverly Hills, (310) 275-5200. Cozy sofas, well-placed table seating areas, polished dark wood bar and lovely murals add to the comfort and style of this great intermission between Rodeo Drive shopping sprees. Full-set menu served daily; great à la carte desserts too.

Westwood Marquis Hotel and Garden, 930 Hilgard Ave., Los Angeles, (310) 208-8765. Before or after UCLA events, stop by this lovely hotel for a full afternoon tea served in the lounge while a harpist plays. Wonderful food and professional staff.

Los Angeles Area

(A word of caution to first-time visitors here; "area" means anywhere from a half-hour to a one-and-one-half-hour car ride from Los Angeles, but to L.A. residents, that's typical. Taxis can devour your budget, so rent a car if you want to explore!)

Chatter, 12424 Ventura Blvd., Studio City, (818) 766-4050. Tearoom and gift shop open Tuesdays through Saturdays, with tea served from twelve noon to three P.M. Loads of fun things to buy, including the cup and saucer you're drinking from. This is a very American, funky place where Doris Day sings and "chatter" is the entertainment.

Elegant Clutter Tea Room and Gift Boutique, 2575 Chino Hills Parkway, Chino Hills, (909) 393-5282. Offers theme teas and traditional afternoon teas with variable schedules and welcomes parties. Great shopping.

Frills Tea Room and Vintage Boutique, 504 S. Myrtle Ave., Old Town Monrovia, (818) 303-3201, and 28535 Front St., Old Town Temecula, (909) 699-6996. Afternoon tea in a charming vintage-clothing store (Monrovia) or Victorian home (Temecula) where you can cop a hat from the wall and play dress-up no matter how old you are. Carefully created menu items to please the palate of any age.

Huntington Library and Botanical Gardens, 1151 Oxford Rd., San Marino, (818) 683-8131. Set in the Rose Garden Room with bucolic views of the surrounding gardens. English-style tea is served buffet-style daily except Mondays. Adjacent to the Library, with its genuine Shakespeare folios, Gainsborough paintings and many other fine art and accessory items.

Past Tyme Tea Parlour, 6553 Greenleaf, Whittier, (310) 945-9462. Seasonal theme teas and twilight teas held throughout the year plus their traditional afternoon tea, served Tuesday through Saturday, are part of the charm of this shop offering antiques, collectibles, gifts and cards.

The Ritz-Carlton Marina del Rey, 4375 Admiralty Way, Marina del Rey, (310) 823-1700. Served in the richly appointed library bar weekends, this tea includes classic Ritz-Carlton tea foods.

The Ritz-Carlton Huntington Hotel, 1401 S. Oak Knoll Ave., Pasadena, (818) 568-3900. A panoramic view of the carefully sculptured Horseshoe Gardens and the city of San Marino is part of the pleasure of afternoon tea here in the lobby lounge, served daily from a choice of three menus.

The Ritz-Carlton Rancho Mirage, 68-900 Frank Sinatra Dr., Rancho Mirage, (619) 321-8282. Lobby Lounge is the scene for fashion teas, art and fine jewelry teas and children's teas plus regular teatime. Pianist. Several menus offered. As with all Ritz-Carlton hotels, sign up for special December Teddy Bear "teas."

The Rose Tree Cottage, 824 E. California St., Pasadena, (818) 793-3337. Complex of storybook thatched-roof cottages offer everything imaginable for gifts and home accessories from England plus one of the best English-style teas anywhere, served on crisp linens with freshly brewed teas and genuine clotted cream for the scones.

Tea Rose Garden, 28 S. Raymond Ave., Old Town Pasadena, (818) 578-1144. Lovely courtyard with fountain is part of this fragrant full-service flower shop and tearoom specializing in edible flowers used in many foods and as garnish. Unique loose-leaf teas and selections from fine blenders, e.g. Royal Gardens and Wedgwood. Open daily.

Tottenham Court, 242 E. Ojai Ave., Ojai, (805) 646-2339. Gift shop of incredible array of table accessories and personal, food and gift items. Charming original murals on walls depict English scenes. Tea is offered from lunchtime through teatime.

A Touch of Class, 25914 McBean Parkway, Granary Square, Valencia, (805) 259-1625. Sip A. C. Perch teas of Copenhagen and select from four menus. Wednesdays through Sundays; Cream Tea only on Tuesdays. Wonderful shopping and delicious food.

Verna's Off Main, 810 Electric Ave., Seal Beach, (310) 431-3392. Victorian tearoom in a delightful seaside resort offers traditional English-style afternoon tea daily plus an endless selection of gifts to choose for your teapot- and antique-collecting friends.

Victorian Tea Company, 225 W. Tenth St., Long Beach, (310) 437-1933. This renovated home is a charming place to hold tea parties following a variety of themes. By appointment only. Gift shop open 1-5 P.M. weekdays. Offers classes in "The Art of Afternoon Tea" and sponsors annual tea weekend for prospective tearoom owners each August.

Santa Barbara and Orange Counties/Southern California

Four Seasons Hotel/Newport Beach, 690 Newport Center Dr., Newport Beach, (714) 759-0808. The elegant Conservatory Lounge is the place for choosing from three levels of afternoon tea, served Monday through Saturday. An elegant respite from heavy-duty local shopping.

The Ivy Cottage, 4973 Yorba Ranch Rd., Yorba Linda, (714) 693-0531. Theme teas, story time and Sunday teas offered in addition to daily afternoon menus at various seatings served with their own "Ivy Blend" teas or choice of classic loose-leaf teas.

The McCharles House Restaurant, 335 S. "C" St., Old Town Tustin, (714) 731-4063. Family collection of one hundred teacups decorate this 1885 California cottage designed in American Victorian style. Fine dining from a selection of nine tea menus served Tuesdays through Saturdays. Tiny Back Shoppe carries their own brand of teas and tea foods.

The Ritz-Carlton Hotel/Laguna Niguel, One Ritz-Carlton Dr., Dana Point, (714) 240-2000. Easily the favorite choice of visitors to this seaside town. Tea is served in the Library, overlooking the Pacific Ocean; three levels of tea menus served daily.

Memphis

The Peabody Hotel, 149 Union Ave., (901) 529-4000. This is the popular hotel where the mallard ducks have the run of the outdoor fountain (and sometimes the run of the hotel) and eccentric acceptance of friendly fowl is so Southern. The tea, however, is classic, served with inimitable grace and always worth the while. A must-do in Memphis. Served Monday through Friday and by reservation.

New Orleans

Windsor Court Hotel, 300 Gravier St., (504) 523-6000. Soothing music from a chamber ensemble or harpist sets the scene for the elegant Salon, where two full tea menus are served daily as you select from twenty-five loose-leaf teas and a European menu. An Orient Express hotel.

New York

Anglers and Writers, 420 Hudson St., (212) 675-0810. Eclectic home-style restaurant with teeny view of the Hudson River offers delicious fare with their fine selection of teas. Open daily.

Barney's New York has tea service Monday through Saturday at the 660 Madison Avenue store and daily at the 106 Seventh Avenue store. For reservations, call (212) 826-8900 or (212) 339-7300 respectively. These are trendy, fun places to sip a cup of tea following the classic shopping experience that only Barney's offers with such élan.

The Four Seasons Hotel, 57 E. Fifty-seventh St., (212) 758-5700. Softly decorated, the lobby lounge offers a quiet ambience of velvet sofas and chairs that invite lingering to sample the three-course afternoon tea served daily.

The Lowell, 28 E. Sixty-third St., (212) 838-1400. The discreetly situated Pembroke Room, on the second floor, invites assignations and not-by-chance meetings as dowagers, lovers and businesspeople partake of the classic afternoon fare daily.

J. P. Morgan Library, 29 E. Thirty-sixth St., (212) 685-0610. Museum–gift shop–cafe, housed in the former home of one of teadom's most dedicated enthusiasts, offers afternoon tea in the Atrium Garden Court daily. All items à la carte. Museum admission is $5.

The New York Palace, 455 Madison Ave., (212) 888-7000. Two-story vaulted ceiling of the Gold Room suggests a jeweled setting for teas in this Stanford White–designed hotel which serves tea daily.

The Peninsula New York, 700 Fifth Ave., (212) 247-2200. The Gotham Lounge serves tea daily to tourists, natives and lovers of elegant lobby lounges. Choice of several menus and classic English blends of teas.

The Pierre, 2 E. Sixty-first St., (212) 838-8000. Murals are the enchanting backdrop for the wildly eclectic Rotunda, which offers both à la carte and full-set menus daily to tourists and shoppers alike.

The Plaza, 768 Fifth Ave., (212) 759-3000. In the classic Palm Court, tea is served elegantly and with great style daily with a particularly wonderful selection of pastries.

The St. Regis, 2 E. Fifty-fifth St., (212) 753-4500. The Astor Court is banked by flowers and embraced by the sound of a harp or piano, the tiny tables festooned with Limoges china and Porthault linens, and the classic tea menu comes with your choice of eighteen teas. Served daily.

T Salon & Tea Emporium, 142 Mercer St., (212) 925-3700. Unique tea showcase set below the Guggenheim Museum Soho in a vast (4,500 sq. ft.) emporium with tea bar, retail tea and gift shops, antique furnishings and a menu as innovative as the setting. Many brands and loose leaf teas, and their own brand of teas that are particularly fragrant and unusual. Full set menus served day and night daily and all food items are made with tea!

The Stanhope Hotel, 995 Fifth Ave., (212) 288-5800. Small Tea Salon offers elegant china, choice of eighteen teas, restful interior design for a lovely afternoon tea experience available daily.

Tea Box Cafe in Takashimaya, 693 Fifth Ave., (212) 350-0100. Modern cafe in exquisite store features charming Japanese items for a few dollars to antiques for thousands. Exceptional menu of fine teas from around the world and exceptional Bento box of tea foods designed like sushi but made of western style foods. Monday through Saturday.

Ten Ren Tea and Ginseng Company, 75 Mott St., (212) 349-2286. Here's the ideal place to sample the world's finest oolongs plus some exceptional greens. Priced per sampling, and everything is available for take-home purchase. An incredible selection.

Toraya, 17 E. Seventy-first St., (212) 861-1700. A gift box of a shop showcasing Japanese sweets: *wagashi* and *goshikito*. Teas by the cup. Setting is restful and quiet under a skylight covering a minimalist architectural interior design. A marvelous find for those who love native Japanese green teas.

Trois Jean, 154 E. Seventy-ninth St., (212) 988-4858. Mariage Frères teas and attention to detail are all part of the exquisite pleasure of this wonderful restaurant. Elegant pastries and pots of tea are all perfectly wonderful.

Waldorf Astoria, 301 Park Avenue, (212) 355-3000. In a small alcove off the main lobby, called Peacock Alley, you'll find a three-course tea, a charming pianist and friendly service in this venerable hotel, formerly two great institutions (the Waldorf and the Astoria) built in the 1890s. Served Monday through Saturday.

Philadelphia

The Bellevue Hotel, 1415 Chancellor Court, (215) 893-1776. Take tea in the elegant Barrymore Room (named for the famous Philadelphia acting family) and enjoy the sophisticated, historic building, one of many homages to our country's past. Tea served daily.

Four Seasons Hotel, 1 Logan Square, (215) 963-1500. You might want to segue from tea to the dining room, where the world's finest chefs are creating sumptuous meals truly fit for any gourmet you might know. Tea is no exception. Served Monday through Saturday in the lobby lounge.

Phoenix

The Arizona Biltmore Resort, Twenty-fourth St. and Missouri, (602) 955-6600. A harpist plays in the Sun Room as you sip tea and nibble on scones Monday through Friday in this venerable Phoenix resort, home to golfers, tennis buffs and sun worshipers.

The Phoenician, 6000 E. Camelback Rd., (602) 941-8200. Easily Arizona's most gorgeous showplace of a hotel, the Lobby Tea Court is a perfect respite that offers a perfect pianist to accompany tea served daily.

Portland

Heathman Hotel, 1009 S.W. Broadway St., (503) 241-4100. The city's most elegant hotel serves tea daily in its Heathman Dining Room.

St. Louis

The Ritz-Carlton, St. Louis, 100 Carondelet Plaza, (314) 863-6300. A classic hotel serving tea in style daily in the sumptuous lobby lounge.

San Diego

Horton Grand Hotel, 311 Island Ave., (619) 544-1886. Completely furnished in Victorian furniture, this historic building is the perfect setting for full tea or cream tea, served Tuesday through Sunday.

U.S. Grant Hotel, 326 Broadway, (619) 232-3121. Relax in richly appointed lobby with highly polished mahogany furniture and fine accessories. Pianist. Tea served Tuesday through Saturday. Located across from Horton Plaza shopping center.

Westgate Hotel, 1055 Second Ave., (619) 238-1818. Traditional hotel lobby offers exceptional full-set tea with choice of twelve teas Monday through Saturday.

San Diego Area

The L'Auberge del Mar Resort and Spa, 1540 Camino del Mar, Del Mar, (619) 259-1515. Lobby lounge with pianist for entertainment at tea, served weekdays only.

San Francisco

The Clift Hotel, 495 Geary St., (415) 775-4700. A perfect spot for full or light tea before the theater, served in the lobby bar with velvet and chintz to comfort you.

The Fairmont Hotel, 950 Mason St., (415) 772-5000. Harpist or guitarist plays in a lobby lounge resplendent with velvet red chairs and the luxury of a full tea menu served daily.

Imperial Tea Court, 1411 Powell St., (415) 788-6080. The first traditional Chinese teahouse in the United States, this classic shop has rosewood and silk-covered walls, classic Chinese rosewood furniture and beautiful traditional lanterns cut from one piece of wood, in the old style. Sells more than two hundred varieties of pure China teas in bulk or packages, tea and herb bath sachets and Pure T ice cream. Tea tastings are kung-fu-style and priced per person. Here's the place to educate your senses and palate on fine China teas daily.

King George Hotel, 334 Mason St., (415) 781-5050. This London-style hotel's Bread and Honey Tea Room on the mezzanine is funky and charming, and the tea foods are great, from the light Hampshire Tea to the substantial Ploughman's Platter. Good stop before the theater.

Mandarin Oriental Hotel, 222 Sansome St., (415) 885-0999. Enjoy English cream tea or traditional afternoon tea with unique tiny quiches, homemade scones and rose petal jam, weekdays in the lobby lounge.

Mark Hopkins Inter-Continental Hotel, 999 California St., (415) 392-3434. This famous hotel at the top of Nob Hill offers full afternoon tea daily served on exquisite accessories and china at beautiful tables.

The San Francisco Marriott Hotel, 55 Fourth St., (415) 896-1600. From its thirty-ninth-floor location, view the Pacific Ocean and Alcatraz as you dine on excellent French pastries and full-set tea served weekdays in the Cocktail Lounge.

Neiman-Marcus, 150 Stockton, (415) 362-3900. The Glass Ship dome ceiling on the top floor is the perfect screen for a sun-splashed afternoon tea served in the Rotunda Restaurant Monday through Saturday at this classic department store. Incredible desserts! Nearby food and gift shop offers many teatime delights.

Park Hyatt Hotel, 333 Battery St., (415) 392-1234. Sumptuous afternoon tea meal served daily in the business-style modern lobby. Pianist plays to soothe the weary business or pleasure traveler.

The Ritz-Carlton San Francisco, 600 Stockton St., (415) 296-7465. Soft silk sofas, cozy eating areas, harpist or other musicians and exquisite furnishings, paintings and soft lighting all make for an exceptionally fine ambience in which to nibble away at this classic afternoon tea. Offered in the step-up lobby lounge daily.

Sheraton Palace Hotel, 2 New Montgomery St., (415) 392-8600. The Republic of Tea is now being served in the hotel's spectacular Garden Court, which sits under a glass dome of seventy thousand panes of etched glass. Music accompanies your choice of three menus served Monday to Saturday.

Stouffer Renaissance Stanford Court Hotel, 905 California St., (415) 989-3500. This former 1876 mansion of Leland Stanford is part of the National Trust and is just the beginning of a delightful afternoon. À la carte or full-set menu served daily.

The Westin–St. Francis Hotel, 335 Powell St., (415) 397-7000. The dark Byzantine Compass Rose Room offers a pianist, a full bar and a comfortable mix of Oriental accessories and English-style sofas and table seating areas for its afternoon teas served Monday through Saturday.

San Francisco Bay Area

Lisa's Tea Treasures, 1151 Minnesota Ave., San Jose, (408) 947-TEAS. Offers eight tea menus at three seatings in an old Victorian house along with countless teas, gift ideas and accessories. Lisa's tearooms are in Lafayette, Pleasanton, and Los Gatos, California, as well as Colorado, Illinois and in other states in the country.

Lady Pierrepont's Heirlooms & Edibles, 1205 Howard Ave., Burlingame, (415) 342-6065. This converted Victorian home is the place to visit when in the Bay Area, set as it is in the charming carriage-trade town of Burlingame, a mecca for antique lovers and gift shoppers. The tearoom offers books, gifts, teas and wonderful accessories that you can view after sampling one of their three tea menus, served Tuesday through Saturday. Fortnum & Mason Royal Blend is the house tea, although many other choices are available.

Stanford Park Hotel, 100 El Camino Real, Menlo Park, (415) 322-1234. Parties of up to one hundred or tea *à deux* are welcomed in the Palm Cafe, overlooking a lovely courtyard. Full-set tea Wednesday through Saturday.

Tea & Crumpets, 817 Fourth St., San Rafael, (415) 457-2495. This on-site crumpet bakery offers a surprisingly sophisticated selection of fine packaged teas and premier selections from Ten Ren Tea Company and other local suppliers of fine loose-leaf teas. The crumpets are truly yummy.

Seattle

Teahouse Kuan Yin, 1911 N. Forty-fifth St., (206) 632-2055. An homage to the goddess of mercy, Ti Kuan Yin, plus an eclectic amalgam of treasures from world travels make this a very special place. The teas are superb, the foods simple and delicious. A marvelously relaxing place for those who truly enjoy teatime for the tea itself.

The Teacup, 2207 Queen Anne Ave. North, (206) 283-5931. It takes courage to open a teashop in the middle of coffee-soaked Seattle, but Cyrus and Mary Noe understand that latte is not for everyone. They offer premium selections for tasting and for take-home plus wonderful accessories. Great mail order source too.

Washington, D.C.

Four Seasons Hotel, 2800 Pennsylvania Ave., N.W., (202) 342-0444. This hotel is the recipient of AAA's five-diamond rating and is located at the entrance of George-town, with its shopping and tourist delights. Tea served daily with a beautiful garden view from the Garden Terrace restaurant.

Henley Park Hotel, 926 Massachusetts Ave., N.W., (202) 638-5200. Traditional English afternoon tea served daily in the Wilkes Room with working fireplace and classical music to soothe you.

Watergate Hotel, 2650 Virginia Ave., N.W. (202) 965-2300. While Washington movers and shakers plan our future, you can relax in Potomoc Lounge and partake of an elegantly prepared tea, offered here daily.

The Willard Inter-Continental, 1401 Pennsylvania Ave., N.W. (202) 628-9100. Just a block from the White House is the beautifully restored Beaux Arts "new" Willard, which has hosted visitors and natives to D.C. since 1816. You'll love their tea, held daily in The Nest, a former sitting room overlooking the main lobby.

OTHER RECOMMENDATIONS

Angel of the Sea, 5 Trenton Ave., Cape May, N.J., (800) 848-3369. Cape May has a plethora of fine Victorian homes, inns and restaurants, many of which offer tea. This is the grandmom of them all and a great place to savor tea Victorian-style.

Chaiwalla, 1 Main St., Salisbury, Conn., (203) 435-9758. Mary O'Brien offers what must be the very best Darjeelings and other fine Indian teas anywhere. A true aficionado, she offers *chai*, an Indian tea "drink" with cardamom, and her tea treats reflect her interest in Himalayan cultures. A must-see. Ask about her Ashley Falls School-house, her proposed tea learning center scheduled to open in November 1995.

Hotel du Pont, Eleventh and Market Streets, Washington, Del., (302) 594-3100. In this tiny state, where tradition and history are so important, you can always rely on the Hotel du Pont to come through for you with a refreshing afternoon tea, served daily in the lobby lounge.

Directory of Blenders, Wholesalers and Tea Shops

❧ ❧

WHAT'S THE DIFFERENCE?

For several years now, the highest price for a Darjeeling at auction in Calcutta has exceeded ten thousand rupees per kilo, or something in excess of five hundred dollars per pound. The cost to the consumer would run substantially higher, of course. Yet anyone can locate a perfectly drinkable Darjeeling retailing for as little as twenty dollars per pound. This extreme example can be repeated, with varying prices, in the case of almost every noteworthy tea. What's the difference?

To begin with, there is *not* any difference if you can't detect it. High-priced teas are made exclusively for connoisseurs who do appreciate these differences and find them worth the money; they would be wasted on those who have not cultivated a discriminating palate and do not know how to prepare the tea to bring out its qualities.

What gives different teas different qualities? Generally speaking, a tea shrub is plucked about every ten days from early springtime, when it awakens from dormancy, until mid-autumn, when it stops "flushing," or putting out new leaf. The first tea plucked every year—called the spring flush or first flush—always has a more delicate character than any harvested subsequently. Depending on the region's climate, there are easily detectable variations between periods for the rest of the year as well. Teas produced in the most favorable times of the year always sell for more than the others.

Variations also abound within the same harvest from the same estate. On rainy days, for example, allowing the green leaf to dehydrate and go flaccid, which is called "withering" the plucked leaf, obviously takes longer. Leaf from higher elevations or shadier sections of the same tea estate also produce variations in taste. Slight changes in the temperature at which the leaf is fired or the length of time it undergoes manufacture produce different tastes. There may be numerous other differences also, which are harder to account for, not to mention drought, flood, unfavorable monsoons, or a change in the estate's methods or management.

The estate factory packs the batch of tea it produced in a given day or two in chests which are grouped together and assigned an invoice number. These chests make up a "lot" of tea, which is sent to auction, sampled by brokers and sold under the identifying invoice number. The first lot an estate ships each year is invoice 1 and the last may be invoice 1,000 or more; thus, the smaller the invoice number, the earlier in the season the tea was produced.

The fewer chests per lot, the more exceptional the tea. Lots sometimes run to over one hundred chests. This usually indicates a blending of several days' production to compensate for some shortcoming in a particular batch and to attain a uniform quality. When a lot consists of twenty or fewer chests, the chances are good this particular batch of tea turned out well above average and the estate hopes it will command a higher price than if it were blended to raise the quality of other batches. A lot that consists of ten or fewer chests is rare indeed, and it is these which bring the top prices like the $500-plus-per-pound Darjeeling.

Blending may and does occur at every level from the producing factory to the retailer. The commonest word of approbation in a tea taster's vocabulary is "useful," meaning the tea can be used in a blend. A "self-drinking" tea, on the other hand, will stand on its own. Only a small percentage of any estate's production will be deemed self-drinking, and obviously, these finest teas are seldom blended, having much to lose and nothing to gain from it. But this is not to say a "single-estate tea" from the same batch is always the product of a single day's plucking and manufacture, though this may often be the case.

Conclusions? All this background information is unnecessary to appreciate any given tea and is seldom known even to the retailer. But it does help one realize the great gulf separating ordinary and even good tea from the truly fine and sometimes great teas which are produced. Tea packers who aim to sell a tea that's simply "good enough" aim for uniformity of taste. You can count on a Twining tea to taste the same from one season and year to the next, regardless of how many teas they had to blend to duplicate the standard they sell and for which they want to be known. Customers who are looking for the best teas, however, do not expect uniformity of taste from one year to the next, even from the same estate. They expect to discover and indeed are intrigued by the variations natural to tea, wine or any other agricultural product.

Furthermore, prestige has a lot to do with price, in tea as in anything else. A Ceylon tea from a famous growing region like Uva or Dimbulla usually costs more than one just as good which cannot claim so exalted an origin. The most highly reputed garden in Darjeeling in recent years is Castleton, with the predictable result that no Castleton tea is cheap. You must expect to pay about one hundred dollars per pound for really first-rate 1995 Castleton, which translates into only fifty cents a cup. On the other hand, Darjeeling teas by this name do come at different prices, and this calls for real discrimination. Many a Darjeeling at half the price is pretty sure to equal a Castleton retailing at seventy-five dollars per pound. With tea as with wine, there are people who drink names and labels. Price is more a function of scarcity than of value in such cases.

Getting the quality of tea you pay for depends upon your own sophistication. This generally requires a certain amount of time and a certain number of mistakes. It is best to cultivate a relationship with one or several tea purveyors who can guide the development of your taste and education. Only after you know what really first-rate Keemun tastes like and what characteristics to expect and look for can you recognize Keemun which is above or poorer than this quality. Attention is all. Since anything one pays close attention to stays in the memory, one quickly develops the ability to remember various tastes. A favorite tea makes us happy now and twenty years from now through the memory of it. In the meantime that memory becomes an indispensable guide to further explorations.

How to Use This Directory

For the last seven years, as cofounder and editor of *Tea Talk: A Newsletter on the Pleasures of Tea*, I have seen an astonishing growth in the tea industry, with a marvelous turn of events: More people are drinking tea and drinking better teas than ever before. While coffee bars and carts seem to be appearing everywhere, coffee sales are actually decreasing by about 5 percent each year. Taking up the slack is the oldest beverage, and the most popular one in the world—tea. You are in the right time and right place to be involved in tea. Because of relaxed trading with China, increased entrepreneurship the world over and a thirst for the finest teas, Americans now have access to an incredible array of fine teas.

The Directory includes listings for the following categories: teas by blender (brand names); tea wholesalers, tea retailers, tearooms, and mail order sources.

Although we have made every effort to include all the teas blended in America and all those sold in the United States although blended elsewhere, no list, no matter how exhaustive the research, can cover it all.

Consumer's Directory of Teas

The following directory includes two main categories: (1) teas by type and (2) names of tea blenders, retailers, wholesalers and mail order catalog sources, marked with the following codes: (B) Blenders, (O) Other or Mail Order Sources, (W) Wholesalers, (R) Retail Shops.

Every effort has been made to create a listing that is all-encompassing, but of course many may be missing (especially packaged blends); we will try to include even more in our next edition. We also did not hear from some blenders and other sources in time to give a complete list of their teas, so we have listed what information we have as a guide.

Caveat emptor: Fresh greens and delicate white and yellow teas vary greatly from season to season, but the suppliers listed here have established a reputation for consistently fine teas. When buying tea types for the first time, we suggest small quantities, e.g., two ounces for sampling, or buy a sampler pack, as available, or in the shop ask for a taste sample, and make your selections in that manner.

We have broken each tea supplier's teas into the conventional areas of white, green, oolong and black, plus specialty blends as applicable. Yellow and "greenish" teas are so rare, they are not included here, although some wholesalers and entrepreneurs do carry them. The addendum to each listing, "Also Available," lists fruited, scented and flavored teas, packaged teas and any unusual categories of tea "drinks," which we have not addressed.

At last count, there were more than ten thousand known tea types from the *Camellia sinensis* and its many varietals, and the list is growing as more and more varieties are available from China, Ceylon, India and other places throughout the world. You will note a variety of spellings for the same teas; we have elected to keep the spellings noted by the sellers rather than be uniform; our apologies to Mr. Webster.

Enjoy the quest for your perfect cup!

Note: All prices are subject to change.

Ahmad Teas (B)
Gavin Gilbey
PO Box 58-1712
Miami, FL 32556-1712
(305) 232-7772
(Available in many fine English tea/gift shops)

Alexander Gourmet Imports Ltd. (W)
1261 McDougall St.
Windsor, Ontario
Canada N8X 3M6

(519) 258-7551
Fax (519) 258-5182
(800) 678-5603 (U.S.)
The following are loose teas sold in 2 1/2 lb. airtight cello poly bags. Call for price quotes.

GREEN
Gunpowder
Japanese Green
Jasmine

OOLONG
Oolong Formosa

BLACK
Assam OP
Ceylon OP (bags and loose)
Darjeeling
Darjeeling OP
Darjeeling TGFOP
English Breakfast (bags and loose)
Irish Breakfast
Keemun
Kenyan
Lapsang Souchong
Russian

Also Available: Represents Tea Masters of London in all traditional flavors; Tea for Me in Darjeeling, Earl Grey, and English Breakfast plus seven fruited flavors in 12-bag packages, variety of Christmas Tea from Munich and Amsterdam, in tea bags and special tins; Herbal Teazers, tea supplies, tins, European naturally flavored teas (18 varieties), decaffeinated scented and fruited teas; does private label packaging.

American Classic Tea (B)
6617 Maybank Hwy.
PO Box 12810
Wadmalaw Island, SC 29487
(803) 559-0383
Fax (803) 559-3049
(800) 443-5987
Mail Order List

The only tea grown in the U.S., American Classic is a mild, clean-tasting tea available in boxes of 20 tea bags and or in loose-leaf form in half-pound tins. They also carry tagless iced tea bags and American Classic Tea Sampler, Tea Jelly, Benne Wafers. May be ordered directly or from Robert & Joseph, Simpson & Vail and other fine purveyors.

American Tea Masters Association (O)
41 Sutter St., Box 1191
San Francisco CA 94104
(415) 775-4227

Each month the association selects a limited-production premium China tea for distribution to participants in the Master Select Series Program. Series subscription is $75 per month plus a 15 percent surcharge for nonmembers. Individually selected China teas are from $100 to $3,000 per pound and rarely are duplicated.

The association of tea connoisseurs, established to promote the art of China tea, provides information, collective purchasing and recognition of achievement to those dedicated to fine rare China tea.

The introductory program for nonmembers includes either a five-class course or single-class course for $400 and $100 respectively. All classes are conducted by a Certified Master of the Association.

Barnes & Watson Fine Teas (B)
1319 Dexter Ave. N., Suite 30
Seattle, WA 98109
(206) 283-6948
Fax (206) 283-0799

Linell Nevins and Leah Grossman have created a very sophisticated line of teas, blending them in small batches for freshness and scoping the world's best sources for a balanced, interesting group of choices. Prices are for 4 oz. of loose tea; each makes about 50 cups.

GREEN
Temple of Heaven Gunpowder Tea, $5.00
Sencha Fukujyu, $5.00
Jasmine Yin Hao, $5.00

OOLONG
Formosa, $5.00

BLACK
Darjeeling Namring, $10.00
Assam Golden Tip, $5.00
Classic Irish Breakfast, $5.00
Classic Earl Grey, $5.00
Classic English Breakfast, $5.00
Queen Victoria's Blend, $5.00

Also Available: Five-scented teas, Classic Blend and Tahitian Blend Iced Tea; decaffeinated teas, tisanes and herbals and European-style gauze tea bags for use in cups; they're reusable and easy to handle. Only Apricot, iced teas, and Classic English or Irish Breakfast and Earl Grey are available in bags.

Barnie's Coffee & Tea Company (B/R)
340 N. Primrose Dr.
Orlando, FL 32803
(800) 284-1416
Fax (407) 898-5341

From India and the Far East to imports from Germany, Barnie's now offers 98 teas, including some with a distinctly Southern flavor, e.g., Peaches-n-Cream and Raspberries-n-Cream. All their teas have been formulated to taste great over ice. Barnie's has 85 stores in 17 states, and its teas and coffees are distributed by Superior Coffee & Foods and Standard Coffee. All the following are for 20 tea bags, unless otherwise indicated.

GREEN
Gunpowder, loose only, $1.79

BLACK
Russian, $2.49
Gold-Tipped Darjeeling, $2.49
Formosa Oolong, loose only, $1.79
English Breakfast, $2.49, and loose, $1.79
Chinese Restaurant, $2.49
Ceylon BOP, $2.49

Also Available: Gift baskets, mugs, flavored teas, loose and 20-bag packages, $1.79 to $2.49, 28 flavors from Ginseng, Cherries-n-Cream to

Coffee Cake, Piña Colada; decaffeinated teas, both traditional and flavored, seven selections.

Barrows Tea Company (B)
142 Arnold
Bedford, MA 02740
(508) 990-2745

Barry's (B)
(Available at most English and Irish food shops)

The Bell Tea of New Zealand (B)
(*See* O'Mona International)

Bencheley's (B)
(*See* Empire Coffee and Tea)

Bewley's (B)
1130 Greenhill Rd.
West Chester, PA 19380

R. C. Bigelow, Inc. (B)
201 Black Rock Turnpike
Fairfield, CT 06432-5512
Mail Order Catalog
(800) 841-8158 (credit card holders only)
For more than 50 years, Bigelow has sold what was probably the first commercially prepared flavored tea, Constant Comment. It's still selling, along with the company's many other flavored teas often displayed in their trademark wooden chests. They do, however, carry some traditional black teas: Earl Grey, English

Teatime and English Breakfast, available at all supermarkets.

Billy Tea of Australia (B)
(Available at most English food and tea shops)

Blue Willow Tea Company
707 E. Pike St.
Seattle, WA 98122
(206) 325-9889
Fax (206) 325-7153
Frank Miller has taken the best teas from Asia, India, and Sri Lanka, packaged them in lovely, recyclable boxes and is helping to turn this coffee city on to tea. Sells wholesale and bulk to restaurants and tea shops. Many accessory items are offered.

Boston Harbour Tea (B)
(*See* Mark T. Wendell, Importer and O'Mona International)

British American Imports (W)
726 Fifteenth St.
San Francisco, CA 94103
(415) 863-3300
Fax (415) 863-1495
Warren Ford's Alice's Adventures in Wonderland and Beatrix Potter teas are available at many English food and gift shops. The lines include ten-bag packages of English Afternoon, English Breakfast and Earl Grey plus Lemon, Strawberry and Apple. Suggested retail

prices, $4. Earl Grey and English Breakfast are also available in loose tea under the Beatrix Potter labels.

Also Available: English tea cosies, tiered stands, Wade English Life collector teapots, novelty teapots, Brown or White Betty teapots.

Brombertee (B)
(Available at most English tea/gift shops)

Burberry's Teas (B)
(Available at most English tea/gift shops)

Camellia Tea Company (O)
PO Box 8310
Metairie, LA 70011-8310
Fax (504) 835-3318
(800) 863-3531
Mail Order Catalog

Barely one year old, Camellia Tea is fast becoming the catalog for "the rest of us" who do not live in major shopping areas. Their carefully selected choices for the afternoon table include fun iced tea accoutrements, elegant one-of-a-kind silver teapots, scrumptious tea table foods and their own line of teas: China Keemun, plus flavored choices of Irish Cream, Mango, Passionfruit and Italian Fruit. Each bag comes with 4 oz. of loose-leaf tea which yields over 60 cups. $5.80 each.

Also Available: Barnes & Watson, Kobos, Eastern Shore, Fortnum & Mason, full line of Republic of Tea, Williamson and Magor, and herbals from MarketSpice (Reg.), Davison's, Dr. Stuart's Botanicals, Select and Alaska Wild Teas.

Canterbury Cuisine (W/B)
PO Box 2271
Redmond, WA 98073
(206) 881-2555
Fax (206) 881-3170

Makers of scone mixes and the new Lat-Tea, a tea version of the famous coffee drink; available at most specialty food and gourmet stores.

Celestial Seasonings Inc. (B)
4600 Sleepytime Dr.
Boulder, CO 80301-3292
(303) 530-5300
Fax (303) 581-1249

In 1994, for the first time, the company known best for herbal teas introduced a line of black teas. All are carefully developed and uniquely designed, available at your local supermarket. The company offers extensive gift packs, tea accessories, factory tours, tea tastings and a tearoom for breakfast or lunch at their Boulder location. All items are available mail order.

BLACK
Ceylon Apricot Ginger
Earl Greyest
English Breakfast
Fast Lane, with ginseng and exotic spices
Firelight Orange Spice

Vanilla Maple
Morning Thunder (with maté)
Misty Mango (with black teas from Assam,
Java and Kenya plus Oolong)
Organically grown Orange Pekoe

GREEN
Emerald Gardens, Chinese green and Ceylon
black teas flavored with plum and passion
fruit

Chaiwalla, The Tea Room
1 Main St. (PO Box 544)
Salisbury, CT 06068
(203) 435-9758
Tea sold by the ounce or by the pot: exceptional single garden Indian teas a specialty.
and

Chaiwalla Fine and Rare Teas (R)
The Ashley Falls Schoolhouse
PO Box 217, 21 Clayton Rd.
Ashley Falls, MA 01222
(413) 229-8088
Fax (413) 229-8099
Tea Order List
Offers primarily India teas from exquisite gardens, plus selected China teas. All prices are for 150 grams, except where noted.

GREEN TEAS
Fine Green Hyson, $8.00
Silver Tips, Minimuttar, $8.00

BLACK
Assam Ethelwold Garden, Kenduguri or
Betjian, $10.00
Assam Hattialli CTC, $8.00
Darjeeling Marybong Garden or Goomtee
Garden, $12.00
Darjeeling Sungma Garden, Teesta Valley or
Selimbong Garden, $10.00 each
Keemun, $7.50
Lapsang Souchong, $6.50
Nilgiri Havukal Estate (200 grams), $9.50

INDIAN SPECIALTIES
Terai, Kamala Garden, $9.00
Banarashi (brewed with cardamom and
vanilla), $10.00
Kashmir Kawab (North Indian tribal tea),
$6.50
Sherpa (Himalayan Climbers Tea), $7.50
Chaiwalla House Tea (milk tea with spices),
$10.00
Also Available: Moroccan Mint, B&B Spice Tea,
Chamomile (50 grams), and glass museum
teapots and accessories.

Chandlers Teas (B)
(Available at most English and Irish tea and
food shops)

Coffee Bean and Tea Leaf
630 Colorado Blvd.
Camarillo, CA 91204
(805) 484-7924 or (805) 389-9610

Extensive line of loose-leaf teas sold primarily in their more than thirty retail shops, based in California. Call for selection list.

Corti Brothers (R/W)
5810 Folsom Blvd., PO Box 191358
Sacramento, CA 95819
(916) 736-3800
Fax (916) 736-3807
Newsletter

This grocer and wine merchant has been offering the finest olive oils, wines, bourbons and delectables since 1947. Now co-owner Darrell Corti has discovered the pleasures of tea and is the exclusive agent in this country of Hong Kong merchant Wing-Chi Ip, owner of the Lock Cha tea shops. Teas from the Zhang family gardens are often separated into single-day harvests (SDH). The plucking for the day is processed and the final tea is done about 12 hours later. Choices are in limited quantities and vary greatly from season to season. CFQ (call for quote) on late arrivals. All teas are sold in 2 and 4 taels; we list prices for 2 taels (76 grams).

WHITE
Shoumei, $4.90
Fuding Silver Needle, $16.20

GREEN
Longjing, Meijiawn area of Hongzhou, CFQ
Longjing, #43 clone, Tea Research Institute, CFQ
Bi Lo Chun, Dongshon area of Suzkow, CFQ

OOLONG
Golden Cassia, $4.90
Hairy Crab, $4.90
Hairy Crab SDH (A), $7.09
Hairy Crab SDH (B), $8.60
Autumn Harvest, Tieguanyin (CFQ)
Tieguanyin SDH (A), $10.79
Tieguanyin SDH (B), $16.20

Davison Newman (B)
(*See* O'Mona International *and* Mark T. Wendell Co., Importers)

Dean & Deluca (R)
560 Broadway
New York, NY 10012
(212) 431-1691
Fax (212) 334-6183
Mail Order Catalog of complete line of foods and beverages
and
3276 M St., NW, 1299 and 1919 Pennsylvania Ave., NW, in Washington, D.C., plus the following locations where tea is served daily: 1071 Fifth Ave., 235 W. 46th St., 121 Prince St., 9 Rockefeller Center, 75 University Place and 1 Wall Street Court in New York, NY; 251 S. 18th St., 1601 Market St. and 4311 Main St., Philadelphia, PA.

This fabulous purveyor of fine foods and beverages has the best of everything and everything of the best. In addition to many standard packaged teas and brand-name connoisseur teas (see below), they carry Teas Kousmichoff (Kusmi). Available in 25 muslin bags, $8.85, or loose leaf, 3.5 oz., $6.35, including Ceylon Extra, Toika (Ceylon, India, Indonesian and China teas), Darjeeling, Evening Russian (Ceylon and China teas) and 14 flavored or scented teas with flower essences, vanilla, citrus and other spices.

Also Available: Barry's, Bewley's Irish, Eastern Shore, Fortnum & Mason, Grace Rare Teas, Harney & Sons, Hu-Kwa, Hyon's, Indar, Jackson's of Picadilly, Le Cordon Bleu, Mariage Frères, Republic of Tea, Roger Vergé, Royal Gardens Tea Company, Simpson & Vail, Sundial, Twinings, Ty-Phoo plus herbals from Shakers, Pompadour, Heath & Heather, Eastern Shore and Dr. Stuart's Botanicals.

Douwe Egberts of Holland (B)
(*See* O'Mona International)

Drysdale's of Edinburgh (B)
(*See* Dean & Deluca *and* O'Mona International)

Duchess of Devonshire (B)
(Sold at most fine English tea/gift shops)

Eastern Shore Tea Company (B)
PO Box 84
Church Hill, MD 21623
(800) 542-6064
Mail Order Catalog
Eastern Shore has created fruited and scented teas which are remarkable because they use full-leaf, excellent teas and superb flavorings rather than fannings and dust or mediocre teas with synthetic flavoring. While the line is primarily unique flavored teas, they do carry a distinguished list of fine unblended gourmet teas, which we list here. All the teas marked (*) are available packed in reusable tea bags (of 3 oz. each) for convenience in brewing inside white, foil-lined bags to ensure freshness; all may be purchased in bulk.

GREEN
Dragonwell, $19.50/lb.
*Dragonwell, $7.95 per 3 oz. pkg. or $19.50/lb.
Gunpowder, $12.50/lb.
Jasmine, $12.50/lb.
Young Hyson, $13.50/lb.

OOLONG
*Ti Kuan Yin, $7.95 per 3 oz. pkg. or $19.50/lb.

BLACK
Assam, $13.50/lb.
Ceylon OP, $12.50/lb.
Keemun, $12.50/lb.
Lapsang Souchong, $13.50/lb.
Rose Congou, $12.50/lb.
Lychee, $12.50/lb.
Yunnan Tea, $13.50/lb.
*Earl Grey, $6.95 per 3 oz. pkg. or $14.50/lb.
*Darjeeling, $8.95 per 3 oz. pkg. or $25.00/lb.

*Kenya, $6.95 per 3 oz. pkg. or $14.50/lb.
*Russian Caravan, $5.95 per 3 oz. pkg. or $13.50/lb.
*Moroccan Mint, $5.95 per 3 oz. pkg. or $13.50/lb.

Also Available: Five herbal blends and 16 flavored black teas from Watermelon-Kiwi to Key Lime Colada to Burgundy Cherry.

Empire Coffee & Tea Company (R)
592 Ninth Ave.
New York, NY 10036
(212) 586-1717
(800) 262-5908
and
231 Washington St.
Hoboken, NJ 07030
(201) 216-9625

Founded in 1908, this shop custom blends and roasts its coffees and offers a choice selection of packaged and loose-leaf teas. Prices are for loose teas in 4-oz. quantities; also available in 1/2 lb. and 1 lb. quantities.

GREEN
Chunmee, $3.25
Dragon Well, $3.85
Green/Black (mixed), $2.80
Gunpowder Green, $4.50
Pan-Fired Green, $3.25

OOLONG
Oolong Fancy, $2.90
Oolong Small, $2.60

BLACK
Assam/Darjeeling, $3.25
Asam India, $2.90
Ceylon Aldora, $2.70
Ceylon Fancy, $2.95
Ceylon Small, $2.60
China Black, $2.75
China Mainland, $3.35
Chinese Restaurant Tea, $2.60
Darjeeling, $3.50
English Breakfast, $2.75
Flowery Orange Pekoe, $3.35
Irish Black, $2.60
Java Superior, $2.70
Keemun, $2.75
Kenya Black (small cut), $2.95
Mixed Black, $2.60
Orange Pekoe (New York Blend), $2.60

SPECIALTY
Earl Grey, $2.75
Jasmine, $2.60
Jasmine Spice, $2.70
Lapsang Souchong, $3.30
Lychee Black, $2.80
Rose Black, $2.70
Russian Black, $2.70
Russian Wine, $2.75

Also Available: Flavored and scented loose-leaf teas; packaged teas from Bencheley and Bencheley Decaf, Twinings of London, and Stash; herbals from Breezy Morning, Celestial Seasonings, Pompadour, Health Tea and Yerba Mate from Argentina, and many others.

Empire Tea Services (W/R)
5155 Hartford Ave.
Columbus, IN 47203
(800) 790-0246 or (812) 375-1937
Fax (812) 376-7382

Fine teas have come to the Midwest thanks to the owners of Empire, who have both a tearoom at the Columbus Inn and sell a line called Guy's Tea, tea bags in wood boxes, blended exclusively with Ceylon tea. The 20-bag boxes come in Ceylon Supreme, English Breakfast and Earl Grey plus seven fruited flavored teas. Suggested retail, $4.

Equator Estate Coffees & Teas (MO/W)
5645 Paradise Dr.
Corte Madera, CA 94925
(800) 809-POUR (7687)
Mail Order Catalog

This brand-new mail order company is specializing in rare cargo collection teas, many limited edition estate teas from Mainland China, and will offer a Tea of the Month that is an estate tea. They do private labeling and personally blend teas to suit. Because the teas are seasonal, prices will vary. All teas are loose leaf. Will soon add some name-brand packaged teas to their carefully chosen lists.

Fanci Premium Tea Company (B)
PO Box 14351
San Luis Obispo, CA 93460
(805) 543-8200 or (800) 542-8200
Fax (805) 544-5142

This fine new tea company has an excellent line of packaged teas, using Ceylon teas, plus a very carefully selected list of fine teas from around the world that is available wholesale by the pound to retailers and retail by the ounce to consumers.

The following are retail prices per ounce:

GREEN
Dragonwell, $1.29
Gunpowder, $1.29
Gunpowder #1, $1.29
Sencha, $1.86
Young Hyson, $0.69

OOLONG
Oolong Choice, $1.44

BLACK
Assam TGBOP, $0.96
Ceylon Supreme, $1.47
Chester, $0.54
Darjeeling TGFOP, $1.65
Darjeeling TGBOP, $1.29
Kalgar, $0.75
Kenya, BOP, $1.02
Lapsang Souchong, $1.05
Lychee, $0.87
Orange Pekoe, $1.11
Supreme (Ceylon), $0 .72

Also Available: Bulk tea in blends ($0.69 to $0.90 per 1 oz.), scented ($0.90 per oz.), decaffeinated ($1.38 per oz.) and teas in four flavors, $3.49 per 12-bag package.

First Colony Coffee & Tea Company
(W)
Norfolk and San Francisco
PO Box 11005
Norfolk, VA 23517
(800) 446-8555

This wholesale tea company offers both a line of flavored teas (Susan's Tea) and an exceptional collection of traditional teas for the gourmet food or specialty shop. They are available in bulk, 12 four-oz. envelopes and tins of 25 tea bags each.

GREEN
Gunpowder
Pan-Fired Green
Pinhead Gunpowder
Young Hyson

OOLONG
Black Dragon

BLACK
Assam
Ceylon Orange Pekoe
Darjeeling TGFOP
Earl Grey
English Breakfast
Gold-Tipped Darjeeling
Irish Blend
Keemun
Lapsang Souchong
Pingsuey

Queen's Blend
Russian Yunnan Black
Yunnan Tipped Black

Also Available: Flavored, Decaffeinated and Decaf Flavored plus tea samplers for regular and flavored teas. Also sells Susan's Tea, a line of flavored tea-bag teas.

Flower Cup (MO)
(*See* Schapira)

Fortnum & Mason (B)
(Available at most English food and gift shops)

Four O'Clock Tea Co.
PO Box 641
Ellington, CT 06029
(203) 872-1505

Choose from gift bags of twenty bags of Royal Windsor, Mango Indica, Victorian or Regency Earl Grey.

Freed, Teller & Freed (R)
1326 Polk St.
San Francisco, CA 94109
(415) 673-0922
Fax (415) 673-3436
Mail Order Catalog
For all phone orders, refer to numbers above
and

Embarcadero Center/West Tower
San Francisco, CA 94111
(415) 986-8851
Fax (415) 986-8853
Outside San Francisco (800) 370-7371

Since 1899 this venerable purveyor of coffee and tea has provided the very best in teas and tea accessories. Offers mail order, plus two shops in San Francisco. Freed's has become a benchmark of what a fine tea shop should be: well-trained and informed staff selling the finest teas in the world. The following are teas usually in stock; for unusual teas or seasonal selections, please call on availability.

All teas listed below are sold in 1 lb., 8 oz. and 4 oz. sizes; we list the 4 oz. size only. All teas are loose leaf.

GREENS
Green Japan, $1.25
Spider Leg, $2.75
Gyokuro Asahi, $12.50
Gunpowder—Temple of Heaven, $2.75
Dragon Well—Lung Ching, $10
China Jasmine, $2.25
Jasmine Yin Hao, $6.25
Jasmine Dragon Pearls, $10

OOLONGS
Formosa Oolong, $2.75
Oolong, Fancy, $11.50
China Oolong—Tai Quan Yin, $4.25

BLACK TEAS
Darjeeling Deluxe, $7.50
Darjeeling First Flush, $8.75
Darjeeling Fancy, $18.75
Assam FOP, $2.50
Assam Fancy, $6.25
Nilgiri, $2.00
Orange Pekoe (Ceylon), $2.50
China Keemun, $22.25
Keemun Deluxe, $3.75
Keemun Hao Ya-A, $7.50
Yunnan, $2.00
Lapsang Souchong, $1.75
Golden Ceylon BOP, $2.25
Himalaya Rose BOP, $2.25
Assam (BOP), $2.00

BLENDED TEAS
Earl Grey, $2.75
English Breakfast $2.50
Irish Blend, $2.50
Samovar Blend, $2.50
Russian Caravan Blend, $2.50

Also Available: Decaffeinated, herbals and flavored teas, many tea accessories including Swiss Gold Teapot Infuser, teapots, tea table foods.

Golden Moon Tea, Ltd. (B)
PO Box 1646
Woodinville, WA 98072
(206) 869-5376
Mail Order List

This relatively new firm (opened in 1994) pledges no soggy paper tea bags, no processed decaf or trendy herbals, only true tea from the *Camellia sinensis* bush, and they've selected a remarkably fine list for their premier inventory. Available in airtight tins that contain 4 oz. each. They do offer bulk teas to consumers and can sell wholesale to gourmet and specialty retailers.

WHITE
A rare white tea with chrysanthemum flower, $9

GREEN
Japanese Sencha, $11.95

BLACK
Tippy Earl Grey, $7.95
French Breakfast (Kenilworth Ceylon), $12.50
Rose, $7.95

SPECIALTY
Vanilla Jasmine (black tea, jasmine tea and petals, vanilla pieces), $11.00
Pu-Erh, $9.00

Also Available: Sampler packs for wholesalers and for retail customers. Please call for quotes.

Grace Rare Teas (B)
Grace Tea Company, Ltd., New York
50 West 17th St.

New York, NY 10011
(212) 255-2935
Mail Order List

The elegant black tins with superb teas are Grace's signature. Hardly a year goes by that a new award does not honor Before the Rain Jasmine or Winey Keemun. For 30 years Marguerite and Richard Sanders have sought the finest teas from Taiwan, China and Hong Kong and their unsurpassed quality is uniform in every cup, a sure sign of the hand-blending and hand-packing of their teas. Each tin holds 8 oz.

GREEN
Pouchong "Before the Rain" Jasmine, $11.25
Pinhead Gunpowder Pearl, $10.55

OOLONG
Formosa Oolong Supreme, $12.95

BLACK AND BLENDS
China Yunnan, $11.25
High-Grown Fancy Ceylon, $11.25
Pure Assam Irish Breakfast, $11.25
Superb Darjeeling 6000, $11.25
Winey Keemun English Breakfast , $10.55
Lapsang Souchong Smoky No.1, $10.55
Russian Caravan, $10.55
Earl Grey Superior Mixture, $10.55
Connoisseur Tea Special Blend, $11.05
Demitasse After Dinner Tea, $11.25

Also Available: Superb Egyptian Camomile and

Pure Peppermint, teapot teabags for Winey Keemun, Earl Grey Mixture and Connoisseur Blend.

Guy's Teas (B)
(See Empire Tea Services)

Harney & Sons (B)
Village Green, PO Box 638
Salisbury, CT 06068
1-800-TEA TIME
Fax (203) 435-5044
Mail Order Catalog

Teas are offered in large hotel-size tea bags, single-serving tea bags and loose teas in tins. Gift packs from $10 to $75 are available as is a Tea of the Month Club, priced from $48 to $204 plus a variety of tea accessories and some tea-table foods.

SPECIALTY TEAS (all sold in 3 oz. loose-leaf packages)
Second Flush Darjeeling, Soureni Garden, $18.00
First Flush Darjeeling, Namring or Dooteriah, $12.00
Yi Hong Keemun, $10.00
Fanciest Formosa Oolong, $10.00
Tippy Yunnan, $8.50
Panyang Congou, $8.50
Assam, TGFOP, Manjushree Garden or Lattakoojan Garden, $12
Assam Golden Tips, Dikom Estate, $25.00

Ceylon, Falcon Garden, $9.50
Kenya, Marinyn Garden, $9.50
Yin Hao Jasmine, $11.75

The following only is sold in 2 oz. packages:
Ceylon Vintage Silver Tips, Sapumalkande Garden, $20.00

GREEN
Gunpowder Green, Anhui Province, $8.75/100-cup loose tea in tin
Sencha, $8.75/60-cup loose tea in tin; 100 hotel tea bags, $12.50
Lung Ching, $12.50/40-cup loose tea in tin
Gyokuro, $13.75/40-cup loose tea in tin
Genmaicha, $8.75/60-cup loose tea in tin
Spring Spear Tips, $25.00/40-cup loose tea in tin

OOLONG
Formosa (Taiwan)
Available in bags, hotel tea bags and loose tea in 90-cup tins, priced $3.50 to $12.50
Special Blend of Formosa Oolong and Jasmine, 90-cup tin, $8.75

BLACK
English Breakfast, Irish Breakfast, Orange Pekoe (Ceylon and India), Lapsang Souchong, Palm Court Blend, Queen Catherine's Blend, East Frisian Blend, priced $3.50 to $12.50 and available in tea bags, hotel tea bags and loose tea in tins. Queen

Catherine's Blend, honoring Catherine of Braganza of Portugal who elevated tea drinking in England when she married King Charles, is available only in 40-cup tins, and the East Frisian Blend, served with cream and candied brown sugar, is available only in 100-cup loose tea in tins.

PROPRIETARY BLENDS
Teaneck Tea (B)
Specially created for the Whittier School in Teaneck, NJ, for teacher Roseanne Ponchick. This mango-flavored tea is sold by the children as a fund-raiser for the school. The children, second graders, learn everything from geography to mathematics from the colorful tea tags they have collected, an ongoing class project that began when some student once asked, "How much is a million?" Profits go to the library of the school. Sold in 25-bag packages for $5 each. (Yes, they have surpassed the millionth tea tag, but the fever of collecting, and learning, goes on with each successive second grade class, thanks to Ms. Ponchick's enthusiasm.)

MALACHI MCCORMICK'S BLEND
Blended in honor of author McCormick (*A Decent Cup of Tea*); a rich, satisfying cup of tea. Available in 40- and 100-cup tins, $4.50 and $8.75.

Also Available: Naturally flavored black teas, decaffeinated teas, tisanes (herbals), gourmet iced teas in Plain Pekoe and fruited flavors.

The G. S. Haly Company (W)
611 Veterans Blvd., Suite 210
Redwood City, CA 94063
(415) 367-7601
Fax (415) 367-0291

Since 1889 G. S. Haly has been importing many of the finest teas sold in America. If you want to go into the tea business, this is the wholesaler to note, but be prepared to buy in chest quantities (from 10 to 100 lbs.) appropriate for tea blenders. If you want to create some proprietary blends, this is also a good place to start. Owner Mike Spillane, who learned the business from his mother and now works with his sister, Mary Westjohn, can help you educate your palate and your head. Your first step should be to buy the reprint of the most venerable of all tea tomes, the two-volume set *All About Tea*, by William H. Ukers. The statistics may be off after 60 years, but the main facts remain, and it's a vital addition to any tea importer–retailer–blender's library. Call for price quotes.

The following is only a partial inventory list, and much of the availability depends on the season. Wholesale prices are from $1.10 to $54 per pound and are subject to change; we list choices here rather than prices because of the variance in chest weights and availability.

GREEN
Young Hyson
Dragon Well (Lung Ching finest grade and pan-fired leaf)
Gunpowder #1 (China or Taiwan)
Jasmine Yin Hao, first grade
Jasmine
Pan-fired Taiwan Green
Temple of Heaven Gunpowder
Gyokuro Asahi
Sencha (Spiderleg)
Genmai Cha (blended with roasted rice)

OOLONG
Fanciest, silver tipped
Choicest, silver tipped
Standard

BLACK
Kenilworth Ceylon
Chester Ceylon
Supreme Ceylon
Darjeeling (FTGFOP, TGFOP, TGFOP Fancy, and TGBOP)
Assam (TGFOP and TGBOP)
Kalgar
Nilgiri
Keemun
Yunnan FOP
Lychee
Rose
Lapsang Souchong

Also Available: Yunnan Tea Bricks, Gold English tins, decaffeinated, scented and flavored teas, all made with fine Ceylon, China or Taiwan teas, as requested.

Hawaiian Salrose Teas (B)
1200 College Walk #118
Honolulu, HI 96817
(808) 531-4088
Fax (808) 531-4030
Five exotic-flavored teas: mango, guava, papaya, tropical blend and á laite.

The House of Tea (R)
720 S. Fourth St.
Philadelphia, PA 19125
(215) 923-8327
(800) 923-TEAS
Mail Order Catalog
Cordon Bleu-trained chef Nat Litt has carefully and judiciously collected an astonishing variety of excellent teas, some 200 at last count, and more coming in each day. As a superb chef, who has developed wonderful recipes using tea as a condiment or ingredient, Litt offers variety, freshness and, best of all, very reasonable prices. Visit his shop in Philadelphia or order your favorite selections by mail.

GREEN
Chun Mee Green
Pinhead Gunpowder, special grade

Go Jiang Mao Jian
Young Hyson Green
Spring River Pan Fired
Lung Ching, special grade
Lung Ching, first grade
Lung Ching, third grade
Pi Lo Chun
Green Darjeeling
Green Kangra Hyson
Green Nilgiri, Super Peko
Gen maucha
Gyokuro
Kukicha
Sencha
Bancha
Bancha Twig

BLACK TEAS
Lu Mudan
Black Mudan (Red Peony)
Ceylon BOP
Flower Orange Peko
Keemun Black, first grade
Keemun Black, Hao Ya "B"
Rose Congou Black
Castleton 1 or 2 Darjeeling
Goomti FTGFOP-l Darjeeling
Putabong FTGFOP 1 Darjeeling
Singuilli Garden Darjeeling
Jungpana Estate Darjeeling
Sikim Temi Estate Darjeeling
Margaret Hope Estate TGFOP-1
Darjeeling

Yunnan BOnay, first grade
Yunnan, FOP

OOLONGS
Min Pei
Ti Kuan Yin, special grade
Ti Kuan Yin Oolong
Seychung Oolong, special
Ti Kuan Yin Special Grade

Also Available: Mudis Teas, Nilgiri and Assams
from India, Ceylons, Flavored black teas, Fruit
blends, and teas from France and Europe
including Fauchons Garden, Grand Bois Cheri,
Marco Polo, Montagne D'or, Podrea, Tzar
Alexandre, Tzar Nickolas and Yunnan Imperial TGFOP, among many others. All teas available in 4, 8 and 16 oz. sizes.

Hu-Kwa Tea (B)
(*See* Mark T. Wendell Co. Importers)

Hyon's (B)
(*See* Dean & Deluca)

Imperial Tea Court (R/W)
1411 Powell St.
San Francisco, CA 94133
(415) 788-6080
Fax (415) 788-6079
After years of exploring China tea on his own,
Roy Fong, with his wife, Grace, opened the first
authentic Chinese teahouse in the U.S., pri-

marily to have a place to invite friends to savor the ever-growing inventory of fine China teas this importer-wholesaler-retailer offers. At the tearoom you can savor tea gong-fu (kung-fu) style with tiny thimble cups and small Yixing pots and enjoy tea the way the ancients did. The inventory is considerably longer than listed here and changes frequently following the numerous trips to China Roy makes each year. Prices below are for 2 oz.; all teas are loose leaf, sold in bulk, but there are numerous Chinese packaged teas for the less adventurous plus novelties such as tea bath preparations.

WHITE
Shou Mei, $3.50
Gong Mei White, $2.87
Yunnan Snow Tea, $8.13
Yinzhen (Silver Needle), $11.00

GREEN
Lu Mu Dan, $16.15
Dragon Whiskers, $16.15
Imperial Dragonwell, $35.00
Bi Luo Chun, $20.00
Long Jing (Dragonwell), $20.00
Jade Fire, $20.00
Eshan Pekoe, $8.67
Sword of the Emperor, $45.63
White Water Green Cloud, $28.15
Wu Xi Hao Cha, $15.00

OOLONG
Monkey-Picked Ti Kwan Yin, $22.50

Green Oolong, $4.75 to $8.50
Phoenix Oolong, $4.75 to $10.63
Yellow Gold, $4.75 to $75.00
Ti Kwan Yin, $6.88 to $8.50

BLACK
Superior Yunnan Black, $8.50
Red Mu Dan, $16.15
Qimen (Keemun), $3.50 to $8.50
Yunnan, $1.50 to $8.50

Also Available: Scented and specialty teas including Jasmine Pearl, Fujian Jasmine, Lychee, Mi Lan and Rose Black, $1.65 to $8.50, and Pu-Erhs from $4.75 to $22.50.

Indar (B)
This exceptional line of packaged teas in beautiful gold and black boxes imported from France is available at many gourmet food shops. (*See* O'Mona International, Mark T. Wendell *and* Dean & Deluca here for direct ordering information)

India Tea Importers (W)
Purveyors of Fine & Rare Teas
PO Box 6583
Pico Rivera, CA 90661
(310) 695-2535
Fax (310) 695-4226
Devan Shah and his family have been in the tea business for several generations and today, his sisters "mind the store" in India while he

sells his exceptional choices of teas here in the United States. Shah recently acquired Chado Tea Room in Los Angeles and is expanding their stellar selection. Shah also carries a wide selection of China teas and Ceylon teas in bulk, and in small to large quantities. The following is his India selection; call for choices from other tea-producing countries. Available in 4 oz., by the pound or bulk (20 lbs. or more)

All prices are for 4 oz. except as noted.

ASSAM
Amandabag Estate TGFOP-1, $2.25/bag
Bargang Estate TGBOP, $1.75/bag
Bhuyanpirh Estate TGFBOP (CL), $1.50/lb.
Bogidhola Estate FTGBOP, $1.50/bag
Dekorai Estate GBOP, $1.50/bag
Diksam Estate TGFOP-1, $2.00/bag
Dinjove Estate FTGFOP-1, $2.00/bag
Halmari Estate TFGOP, $2.50/bag
Mission Hill Estate FTGFOP-1, $1.75/bag
Nokhrov Estate FBOP, $1.50/bag
Seajuli Estate TGFOP-1, $2.00/bag

DARJEELING FIRST FLUSH
Castleton Estate FTGFOP-1 (CH), 2 lb. minimum only
Goomti Estate FTGFOP-1, $4.00/bag
Puttabong Estate FTGFOP-1, $4.00/bag
Singbulli Estate FTGFOP-1 (CH), $3.50/bag

DARJEELING SECOND FLUSH
Badamtam Estate FTGFOP-1, $3.75/bag

Castleton Estate FTGFOP-1, $4.25/bag
Darjeeling FTGFOP-1 In Between, $3.00/bag
Darjeeing SFTGFOP-1 Makaibari Estate, $3.50/bag
Jungpana Estate FTGFOP-1, $5.25/bag
Moondakotee Estate FTGFOP-1, $2.50/bag
Milikthong Estate FTGFOP-1, $2.25
Namring (Upper) Estate FTGFOP-1, 2 lb. minimum only
Namring (Upper) FTGFOP-1, $4.25/bag

DARJEELING AUTUMNAL FLUSH TEAS
Margaret Hope Estate 1994 SFTGFOP-1, $16.00/lb.
Sungma Estate (1993) FTGFOP-1, $12.00/lb.

OTHER DARJEELINGS
Arya Estate FTGFOP-1, $2.00/bag
Snow View Estate SFTGFOP-1, $2.50/bag

NILGIRI
Corsley Estate TGFOP, $2.25/bag
Havukal Estate OP, $2.25/bag
Havukal Estate BOP, $1.75
Pascos Woodlands Estate FOP, $1.75/bag
TigerHill Estate FOP, $2.25/bag

SIKKIM
Temi Estate FTGFOP-1, minimum 2 lbs.

GREEN TEAS
Chamraj Estate Hand Rolled Green Tea, $18.00/lb.

Craigmore Estate Nilgiri Green Tea, $2.00/bag
Dunsandale Estate BPS, $9.00/lb.
Dunsandale Estate FTGFOP, $7.00/lb.
Kangra Green Tea, $3.50/bag

ORGANICALLY GROWN TEAS
Dothu Estate Nilgiri BOP, $6.50/lb.
Pussimbing Estate Darjeeling FTGFOP-1, $10.50/lb.

Also Available: Blended teas, including English Breakfast, Irish Breakfast, an Afternoon Tea blend and a Moonlight Tea blend, flavored teas, decaffeinated flavored teas, and teas from Japan, Ceylon, green, oolong and black teas from China.
Risheehat Estate Darjeeling KGFOP-1, $4.00/bag

The Indochina Tea Company (B)
PO Box 1032
Studio City, CA 91614
(213) 650-8020
Fax (213) 650-8022
Mail Order List
American Gabriella Karsch, who speaks Vietnamese and has immersed herself in the culture of Vietnam for many years, has brought the pleasures of the teas from that country to the American marketplace. Working on this project since 1992, Gabriella is offering teas from the mountains of the North and the Highlands of the South, those are BOP and OP loose-leaf teas grown, processed and packaged in Vietnam.

Available in plug-top tins, bags or boxes; all in 100 grams (3.2 oz.), except as noted.

GREEN
Bac Thai, $4.95, box only
Che Song Hy, 500-gram carton of fifty 10-gram packets; traditionally used with invitation to a wedding, $14.95 box only
Ha Giang (OP), $4.95

BLACK
Che Den (CTC BOP), $3.25
Phu Tho, $4.95, box only
Thac Hoa, $4.95, box only
Tran Phu Tuyet, $11.95

Also Available: Tropicals (Mango, Coconut and Ginger), $5.50 for 100 grams, and Lotus (Che Sen), a Green OP, 100 grams, $6.50.

Jacksons of Picadilly (B)
(Available at most gourmet food and specialty shops)

Kado (R)
The Way of Flowers
2319 N. 45th St., Suite 198
Seattle, WA 98103
(206) 409-0675
All prices below are for per lb. Samplers, 50-

cup fresh packs and 1/2 lb. prices also available. CFQ (call for quote) on other items.

GREEN
Dragonwell Longing, $24.61
Genmaicha, $28.98
Kado Mountain Green, $28.98
Koyama Sencha, CFQ
Silver Blossom Jasmine, $34.20

OOLONG
Puerh, CFQ
Ti Kuan Yin, CFQ
Tung Ting Black Dragon, $47.50

BLACK
Assam, $17.10
Cameronian, $14.73
Ceylon, CFQ
Chai Royale, $23.28
Darjeeling, $22.33
Earl Grey, $15.68
English Brisk, $16.63
Irish Morning Mist, $21.38
Keemun, $15.68
Lapsang Souchong, $14.73

Also Available: Specialty flower teas and herbals, teapots, strainers, muslin tea bags and tea trays. Sampler Boxes are available for black teas (nine), $15.75; greens, (four), $10; India blacks, $10; Chinese (three blacks and one oolong and two greens), $10.50.

Kinnells Scottish Tea (B)
620 W. Seventh Ave., Suite 207
Spokane, WA 99204
(509) 747-9064
(800) 337-4832
Fax (509) 747-4711

Artist-shoemaker Valerie Clausen traveled to Scotland, fell in love with the teas and the 18th-century building housing Kinnells Scottish tea, and is now artist-shoemaker-tea blender! She imports six of Kinnells Scottish Teas and plans three more choices to debut at the 1995 Edinburgh Music Festival. Each tea is available in 2 oz. (25-cup) or 4 oz. (50-cup) sizes in black and red Oriental tins.

Prices below are for 2-oz. tins.

SPECIALTY TEAS
Pouchkine Tea, a refined relative of Earl Grey, $11.20
Duke of Edinburgh, India and China leaves, $7.10
Scottish Breakfast Tea, $6.70
Almond Supremo, Keemun with almonds, orange and citrus petals, $6.70
Mango Superior, Keemun black with citrus and mango, $8.70
Blue Lady Keemun with fruit and blossoms, $6.30

Also Available: Electric stainless steel samovars; French teapots, silver infusers and French Presspots plus samplers and gift sets.

Kousmichoof (Kusmi) (B)
(*See* Dean & Deluca *or* O'Mona International)

Lat-Tea (B)
(*See* Canterbury Cuisine)

Le Cordon Bleu (B)
(*See* Dean & Deluca)

Lindsay's Teas (B/W)
380 Swift Ave., #10
South San Francisco, CA 94080
(415) 952-7057
Fax (415) 952-9284

A division of the venerable San Francisco coffee firm, Mountanos Brothers Coffee Company, the eponymously named company honors Mike Mountanos's daughter, Lindsay. Beautifully packaged, carefully blended, the line of teas comes in round colorful canisters. Blends, fruit teas and tisanes, decaffeinated teas, and iced teas are also available in bulk to retail customers.

The following are each available in packages of 4 oz. of loose tea or 25 round tea bags, respectively.

Earl Grey, $5.90 and $5.50
Ceylon Supreme, $6.90 and $5.50
English Breakfast, $6.80 and $5.50
Matt's Basketball Tea, $8.40 and $6.30
Jasmine, $6.90 and $5.50
Dragonwell, $6.70 and $5.95

Also Available: Earl Grey Decaf, herbals and fruit teas plus such exotics as Cherry Licorice, Honey Ginseng and Apricot, among others; three iced teas in traditional, Very Very Strawberry and Passion Fruit, each with 24 round tea bags. Fine selection of tea gift packs, Chatsford teapots and mugs in white, brown, blue, yellow, green and red and replacement infusers.

Bulk teas are for wholesale only. Packaged in 2 lb. bags and priced per lb. Call for price quotes.

GREEN
Sencha
Jasmine Fancy
Jasmine, Lindsay's Select
Dragonwell (Lung Chin)
Gunpowder #1
Gunpowder, Temple of Heaven
Yin Hao Jasmine
Chunmee Moon Palace
Young Hyson

BLACK
Ceylon Supreme Estate Orange Pekoe
Supreme
Chester
Kenya BOP
Assam TGBOP
Darjeeling TGFOP
Darjeeling TGBOP
Darjeeling FTGFOP

Kalgar
Yunnan Brick Tea
Keemun Congou
Lychee

OOLONG
Fanciest Oolong
Oolong Choice

Lifeboat Tea (B)
(*See* Mark T. Wendell Company, Importers)

LiveChai (TM) (B)
PO Box 7329
Boulder, CO 80306
(303) 442-6556
Fax (303) 786-7304
Chai is an East Indian concoction consisting of black tea brewed with cinnamon, cardamom, cloves, ginger and pepper, sweetened with honey, pure vanilla and milk. While not in the class of tea, per se, it is fast becoming a popular "tea beverage" here in the U.S. Available in two 32-oz. varieties: Traditional Recipe, a ready-to-serve with milk in aseptic boxes, $3.39, and Traditional Recipe Mix, which can be used with rice or soy drinks or milk, $4.49, and an 8 oz. single-serve drink box, $1.19. Available at some supermarkets and many health food stores. A very portable drink.

London Tea Company (B)
(*See* British Wholesale Imports)

Longbottom Coffee and Tea (B)
PO Box 353
Hillsboro, OR 97123
(800) 288-1271
Also Available: CourTisane organic herbal teas

Lyons (B)
(*See* Gourmet Specialties, De Vries Imports)

MacKinlay Teas Ltd. (B)
PO Box 6, 1382 Industrial Park Dr. #3
Saline, MI 48176
(800) Tea For-U
Fax (313) 429-5823

Tea Imperial Brand (B)
Each individually wrapped tea bag contains gourmet teas "distinctively better, conspicuously different." Packed 48 bags to the box. All are suggested retail price of $3.79 and include Darjeeling Premium, Prime English Breakfast, Prime Green National, Ceylon Royal and Decaf Prime English Breakfast.

MacKinlay Gourmet (B)
Offers a line of 25-count tea-bag teas priced at $2.59 per box. Traditional blends include Darjeeling Premium, Earl Grey, English Breakfast, and three decafs and nine flavored teas.

McGrath's Original Irish Blend (B)
(Available at most English and Irish food and gift shops)

MacNab's Tea Room (MO)
PO Box 206
Back River Rd.
Boothbay, ME 04537
(800) 884-7222
Fax (207) 633-4691
Any-Time Tea Catalogue
All teas are packaged in 1 oz. windowed suit-case pkg., $2.95, and 3 oz. one-cup apothe-cary jars, $7.95.

PROPRIETARY BLENDS
State of Maine Tea, MacNab's own blend of black China teas with a hint of Lapsang Souchang
MacNab Blend, exclusively designed by John Harney & Son, with Assam, Ceylon and Yunnan
Formosa Oolong
Keemun (English Breakfast)
India Assam (Irish Breakfast)
Gunpowder and Lapsang Souchong (Colonial Blend)

Also Available: Flower Tea and tisanes; Yorkshire Teas, 40-count tea bags imported from York-shire Dales, England, $7.95; Tea of the Month Club, $110 for 3 oz. each month, mixture of blends and aromatic teas; tea accessories from Catamount Glass teapots to Blue Willow items; infusers, cosies, strainers and teapot cookie cutters.

Mariage Frères (B)
(*See* Dean & Deluca)

MarketSpice (B/R)
PO Box 2935
Redmond, WA 98073-2935
(206) 883-1220
Mail Order catalog
and
Retail Store
Pike Place Market
Seattle, WA
(206) 622-6340
Since 1911 this small tea and spice shop in Seattle's historic Pike Place has offered a large assortment of bulk teas and spices. Its most famous blend is MarketSpice tea, a tea made in small batches and hand-blended with essen-tial oils and spices; however, they have quite a range of high-end top-quality teas which they deem to be the best, freshest and most reasonably priced. The range of black tea prices is from $4 to $75 per lb. Call for price quotes.

BLACK
Canadian Blend
Ceylon BOP
Darjeeling TGFOP
Earl Grey
Formosan Assam Seed
Indian Assam TGFOP
Irish Breakfast

Keemun
Lapsang Souchong
Lychee
Ceylon BOP Decaf
Russian Caravan
Yunnan

GREEN
Jasmine
Japanese Green
Imperial Gunpowder
Chinese Green

OOLONG
Oolong
Oolong Choice

Also Available: Gift baskets, mesh tea balls, pinch spoons, mesh spoons, eight packaged flavored teas, mugs, 39 herbals including Green Mate, Northwest Breakfast Teas in Apple, Earl Grey and Raspberry; Connoisseur's Tea Blend of Darjeeling, Assam and Ceylon, 25 tea bags, $4.95; 3.5 oz., $4.50; MarketSpice Tea, $8.95 per lb.; $4.50 for 24-bag box.

Melrose's (B)
Jacques F. Weber Co. (W)
2845 Polk St.
San Francisco, CA 94109-8303
(415) 474-5343
Fax (415) 864-8761
The Scottish company, founded in 1812 by Andrew Melrose, first gained its fame when Queen Victoria granted it a Royal Warrant in 1837 to supply both tea and coffee to the royal households in Scotland. This warrant is still held. The teas are packaged in tins in loose-leaf quantities of 3.98 oz. and in packages of tea bags of 25 per box. Available at many fine gourmet and food shops, Melrose's offers English Breakfast, Earl Grey, Queen's, Darjeeling, Ceylon Orange Pekoe and Lemon Scented teas.

Monin Inc. (W)
(800) 966-5225
Flavored tea concentrates with China-Oolong, India-Darjeeling and Ceylon teas sweetened with white beet sugar. Peach, Raspberry, Mango, Plain. Use 1 part tea to 11 parts water. (For Monin syrups, contact Victoria's Treasure.)

My Cup of Tea (B)
PO Box 946
Pasadena, CA 91102-0946
Phone/Fax (800) 946-3329
Genuine Ostfriesen tea from the House of Bunting, one of the oldest tea trading houses in the world. Ostfriesland, the tiny state in northern Germany, was the first in Europe to be introduced to tea imported by the Dutch, and they remain the largest consumers—although they are under 2 percent of the population of Germany, they consume more than

25 percent of the country's tea. This tea is excellent with sugar and milk. Packaged loose leaf in 4 oz. bags.

Neighbors Coffee, Tea & Cocoa (B)

PO Box 54527
Oklahoma City, OK 73154
(405) 552-2100 or (800) 299-9016
Fax (405) 232-3729

Jazzy names and flavors mark these teas, available both in bulk (minimum 2 lb. orders) and in 20-bag or 4 oz. tins. Most are also offered in decaf versions. We list the traditional teas and tea blends as follows; suggested retail prices are approximate:

Bags and Loose Leaf Selections: $3.59 and $5.45 respectively
China Flower
Darjeeling
Earl Grey
English Breakfast
Irish Blend

Bulk Selections, $7.95 to $21/lb.
China Flower
China Gunpowder
Darjeeling
Earl Grey
English Breakfast
Irish Blend

Also Available: Nine flavored teas in bags or 4 oz. loose-leaf tins and 25 flavored/scented/fruited bulk teas, many available decaffeinated for additional charge.

Northwestern Coffee Mills (R)

1025 Middle Road, Box 370
La Pointe, WI 54850
(800) 243-5283

Since 1914 this premier coffee and tea specialty store has offered the finest teas using such old-fashioned methods as personal, guaranteed service and low-key approach to business. Each year they continue to add better and better grades as their customer base becomes better acquainted with first-rate tea, and will soon offer teas by estate designation and leaf grade. They blend, spice and flavor their specialty teas at their own Madeline Island facility in La Pointe.

All prices are per pound; available in 4 oz. to 5 lb. sizes.

GREEN
China Temple of Heaven Gunpowder, $9.95
China Young Hyson Panfired Leaf, $9.95
China Lung Ching Dragon Well (First Leaf), $32.65
Japan Gyokuro Asahi Best Japan Green, $39.95
Japan Sencha Leaf (Spiderleg), $12.60

OOLONG
China Ti Kuan Yin, $22.50

Taiwan (Formosa) Standard Large Leaf, $7.50
Taiwan (Formosa) Choice Large Silver Tip, $11.10
Taiwan (Formosa) Fancy Silver Tip, $34.25

BLACK
Ceylon BOP, $7.46
Ceylon OP, $9.65
China Keemun Congou OP, $12.45
China Keemun Hao Ya "B," $19.35
China Yunnan FOP, $8.90
India Assam TGFOP Choice, Second Flush, $10.60
India Darjeeling TGFOP, Second Flush, $12.95
India Darjeeling FTGFOP, Second Flush, $25.50
Kenya Subukia FP, $8.65
Taiwan English Breakfast Keemun Choice, $8.10
Irish Breakfast FOP, $9.85
Russian Caravan BOP, $7.80

Also Available: American Classic teas, China Flowered Tea Bags, decaffeinated tea and spiced and flavored teas.

O'Mona International Tea Co., Ltd. (O)
9 Pine Ridge Rd.
Ryebrook, NY 10573
(914) 937-8858
The very best packaged teas from around the world are always available, an exceptional list of carefully selected loose-leaf teas. Quantities are as indicated.

WHITE TEA
Sow Mee (White Eyebrow), $3.95/3.5 oz.
Silver Needle, $1.75/2 oz.

GREEN
The following prices are for 4 oz. Also available in 1/2 lb. and 1 lb.
Gyokura, $2.70/4 oz.
Young Hyson, $2.70/4 oz.

The following are priced per weights as shown.
Pi Lo Clun, $9.45/3.5 oz. tin
Lok On, $5.95/8 oz.
China Green Tea, $3.55/3.3 oz.
Dragon Well (Lung Ching), $3.60/5.5 oz.
China Jasmine Tea, $6/4.4 oz.
Gunpowder, $3.60/ 4.4 oz.

OOLONG
Fine Formosa Oolong, $2.70/4 oz.
Formosa Pan Fired, $2.20/4 oz.
China Oolong (Black Dragon), $3.50/3.5 oz.
Ti Kuan Yin, $5.95/4.4 oz. tin

BLACK
The following prices are for 4 oz. Also available in 1/2 lb. and 1 lb.
Russia Georgia, $2.75
Persian, $2.70
Turkish, $2.70

Lapsang Souchong, $2.70
Szechuan, $2.75
China Rose, $3.50
Pinsuey, $2.70
China Lychee, $2.70
Ceylon OP Dimbula, $2.80
Argentina OP, $2.10
Golden Kenya FBOP, $2.75
Golden Kenya FOP, $3.30
Sumatra BOP, $2.75
Java FBOP, $2.70
Indonesia, $4.20
Assam, $2.75
Dooars TGFOP, $4.95
Nilgiri FBOP, $5.94
Darjeeling (Gold Tip), $3.30
Golden Nepal, $4.30

The following packages are prices with weights as shown.
China Black Tea, $3.60/3.5 oz.
Pu-Erh, $6/8 oz.
Tuocha (Yunnan), $3.50/3.5 oz.

Also Available: An extensive list of fine packaged teas from around the world: World Sampler of 120 tea bags, $21, or select from The Bell Tea, Smith & Jamieson, Douwe Egberts of Holland, Yamamoto of the Orient, Hoji Cha, Genn-maicha (brown roasted rice tea), Sencha, Tan-ganda Special Blend, Kousmichooff, Davison Newman & Company, Ty-Phoo, Brook Bond P.G. Tips, McGrath's Original Irish Blend, Mel-rose's, Drysdale's of Edinburgh, Mark T. Wen-dell Company (Hu-Kwa Tea), Indar, First Colony Teas, Ridgeways, Fortnum & Mason, Twinings, Jacksons of Picadilly, and herbals: Pages, Bonomelli and Pompadour.

Orchid Noble Teas (B)
Trade Marcs Group, Inc.
55 Nassau Ave.
Brooklyn, NY 11222
(800) 242-6333
(718) 387-9696 in New York
Premium tea from Sri Lanka (Ceylon) are these unblended, single-district teas. Each packaged in either 10- or 25-teabag packages, $2.50 and $4.

BLACK
Dimbula
Neliya
Ruhuna

Pannikin Coffee & Tea (B/R/W)
1205 J St.
San Diego, CA 92101-7082
(619) 239-1257
(800) 232-6482
Fax (619) 239-9344
Pannikin is a retail division of five stores in Southern California in La Jolla, Encinitas, San Diego, Del Mar and Point Loma. It imports and blends its own teas and its traditional and fruited tisanes. It also offers wholesale sales

through its Cafe Moto division, (619) 239-6686. All prices below are for loose-leaf teas in 4 oz. sizes.

GREEN
Anhui Silver Sprout, $3.61
Green Sencha Fukuju, $5.92
Gunpowder, $2.57
Hunan Gu Zhang Mao Jian, $7.08
Jakarta Clove (Gunpowder), $1.58
Japanese Cherry Sakura, $3.80
Moroccan Green Mint, $2.45
Pan-Fired Green, $2.09

OOLONG
Formosa Fanciest Silvertip, $11.74
Fujian Oolong Tikuanyin, $4.26
Orange Blossom Orange, $3.30

BLACK
Assam Fancy (Second Flush), $3.31
Assam FTGFOP1 Tara, $4.12
Ceylon Pekoe Labookelle, $2.09
Ceylon Supreme, $2.15
Ceylon Uwa Highlands, $2.06
China Keemun, $3.12
Darjeeling TGFOP1 (Namring), $6.75
Darjeeling GFOP (Bandamtam), $3.05
Kalgar, $2.31
Kenya Kaproret, $2.98
Yunnan, $3.37
Also Available: Tea of the Month Club, 1/2 lb. of tea, $8.50 per month for a minimum of four months; Gift Club of 4 oz. of tea, $5.75 per month. Indian-style *chai*, and traditionally flavored teas, e.g., Cinnamon, Guangxi Guihua (apricot), Oriental Condiment, Queen Victoria, Russian Blend, Irish Blend, Jasmine, Lapsang Souchong, Orange Spice, English Breakfast and Earl Grey. They also offered flavored teas with fruit and flower extracts and essences and decaffeinated teas from Europe; tea kettles from Copper Simplex, Michael Graves and Copco; teapots from Jena Museum, Bodum and Brown Betty; and various infusers plus other accessories.

Paradise Tropical Tea (B)
1111 Watson Center Rd., Unit A-1
Carson, CA 90745
(310) 834-4400
Fax (310) 834-0300
The pioneer company in flavored iced tea still has the corner on pure flavor, smoothness and no rough aftertaste: These are the Cadillacs of iced teas. Easy-brew box contains four pitcher-size bags, each making 1 1/2 quarts of tea. Flavors are Original Blend, Passion Fruit, Mango, Papaya, Kiwi and Decaf Original Blend. Price is $3.99 per box. Available now at most supermarkets, some MacDonald's restaurants and all fine gourmet shops.

Peet's Coffee & Tea (R)
PO Box 12509
Berkeley, CA 94712

(510) 704-8090
(800) 999-2132, ext. 220
Fax (510) 704-0311
Mail Order List

Tea merchants since 1966, Peet's takes tea buying and selling seriously and offers a carefully chosen inventory of fine single-estate and blended teas. They are available in their Northern California stores and by mail order. All the following are for 4 oz. quantities except where noted.

GREEN

Gunpowder, $3.75
Hubei Silver Tip, $5.75
Long Ching (Dragonwell), $9.25
Jasmine Fancy, $3.75
Yin Hao Jasmine, $7.75

OOLONG

Ti Kwan Yin, $8.25
Oolong Fancy, $5.25
Golden Dragon Oolong (2 oz.), $6.00

BLACK

Darjeeling Choice, $3.25
Darjeeling Fancy, $5.75
Darjeeling Extra Fancy (Chamong Estate), $9.75
Darjeeling Extra Fancy (Jungpana Estate), $9.75
Assam Golden Tip, $3.25
Assam Extra Fancy, $5.75
Nilgiri, $3.00

Sri Lanka (Ceylon), $3.25
Lapsang Souchong, $3.25
Keemun Fancy, $3.25
Yunnan Fancy, $3.25

SPECIALTIES

Anniversary Blend (available Mid-April), $6.75
Pumphrey's Blend, $3.75

Also Available: Blends for English, Scottish and Irish Breakfast, Russian Caravan, Earl Grey, Orange Spice and Black Currant, each $3.25 per 4 oz.

A. C. Perch of Copenhagen Teas (B)
c/o A Touch of Class (R)
Granary Square
25914 McBean Parkway
Valencia, CA 91355
(805) 259-1625

This venerable Danish firm has been blending fine teas for more than 100 years. You can order these teas from A Touch of Class, the exclusive retail purveyor in the U.S.

P.G. Tips (B)
(Available at most English food shops)

Porto Rico (R)
201 Bleecker St.
New York, NY 10012
(212) 477-5421

and
40 1/2 St. Mark's Pl.
New York, NY 10003
(212) 553-1982
Excellent all-around shop for a variety of teas.

James Norwood Pratt Luxuries (MO)
1411 Powell St
San Francisco, CA 94133
(800) JNP-LUXT
Mail Order Catalog

A love of tea is inseparable from a love of beautiful things to look at, handle and put to use. From the world's various tea cultures and traditions, I endeavor to select only the most beautiful and useful objects being produced and offer them at a reasonable price. Not all luxuries are expensive. Others are, including many of the extraordinary teas I select. My aim is to offer not a wide range but an exclusive selection of teas of a quality which cannot be equaled by any other source elsewhere. Such teas are of extremely limited production and are obviously not for everyone. New teas and wares are added frequently.

All prices for 2 oz., except where noted.

WHITE TEA
Silver Needle, $12.00
JNP White Peony, $4.00

GREEN TEA
Dragon Well, $40.00/4 oz.
Liuan Gupian, $11.00

Dragon Whiskers, $16.00
Lu Mudan, $16.00
Eshan Pekoe, $9.00

OOLONG
Monkey-Picked Ti Kuan Yin, $50.00/4 oz.
Green Oolong, $11.00
Fenghuang Dancong, $11.00

BLACK
Keemun Mao Feng, $20.00/4 oz.
Black Mudan Keemun $16.00
JNP Yunnan FOP, $16.00
Junpana Darjeeling Supreme (A JNP Exclusive), $25.00/4 oz.

Also Available: Pu-Er teas, $44 to $88 per lb.; stainless eclectic tea kettle, Yu-xing teapots, kung-fu tea ware (thimble cups, tea boat, tea drainer and implements), *guywan* (covered cups).

Prince of Persia Tea Company (TM) (MO)
PO Box 6
Grass Valley, CA 95945
Mail Order Catalog

GREEN
China Gunpowder, 100 grams in Geisha Tin, $8.00

OOLONG
Oolong, 110 grams in canister, $10.00

Puchong, 85 grams in canister, $10.00
Jasmine, 35 grams in canister, $5.50

BLACK
Assam BOP, 100 grams in gold tin, $6.50
Darjeeling TGFOP, 100 grams in gold tin, $11.00
Malty Assam, 100 grams in gold tin, $8.00
Kalgar, 100 grams in gold tin, $8.00
Lapsang Souchong, 100 grams in tin, $11
Ceylon Supreme, 100 grams in canister, $5.50
Chinese Black Keemun, Darjeeling Supreme, 100 grams in canister, $5.50
Thai Black (King of Siam), 100 grams in canister, $5.50
Ceylon Supreme, Earl Grey with cardamom, 100 grams in canister, $5.50

Also Available: Tea Bars in Long-Ching, Jasmine, Green and Chysanthemum; tea-bag teas; flavored and scented black teas; decaffeinated tea blends, herbals, spiced and fruited blends; teapots, tea balls and infusers, novelty teapots.

Regency Teas (B)
(Available at many fine English and Irish food and gift shops)

The Republic of Tea (R)
8 Digital Dr. Suite 100
Novato, CA 94949
(415) 382-3400
(800) 298-4832
(Available at most fine gourmet shops)

Ridley's Country Teas (B)
(Available at many fine English food and tea shops)

Ridgways Teas (B)
(Available at many fine English food and tea shops)

Robert & Joseph, Ltd. (MO)
6281 Martin Lane
Redgranite, WI 54970-9533
(414) 566-2520 or (414) 566-2275
Uncle Robert Ory and nephew Joseph Kazda decided that accounting and management weren't as exciting or as interesting as tea, and in 1989 opened a strictly mail-order business selling the finest teas they could find. Their hook is handmade tea bags with their deluxe teas, all prepared by hand so that instead of the dust and fannings of conventional tea bags, customers can enjoy the best flavor from the leaves. They even offer the most astonishing bargain of all: 100 tagless heat-sealable bags for $1.98, although we suspect their aim is to get their customers to bag their own teas and save even more money. The teas are the finest and very eclectic choices.

All prices are for 4 ounces.

GREEN
Chun Pu (whitish and green leaves), $6.00
Lunghing (Dragon Well), $3.80
Gunpowder, Special Grade Temple of Heaven, $3.40

Pan-Fired Green, $2.40
Sencha (Spider Leg), $5.30
Jasmine Sunflower, $3.75
Jasmine Chung Feng (Spring Wind),
$7.14

OOLONG
Sechung, $4.00
Formosa Oolong, $4.40

BLACK
Assam (Seajuli) FOP, $3.40
Assam TGFOP, $4.40
Ceylon (Pettiagalla) TGFOP, $4.30
Darjeeling FOP, $3.20
Darjeeling TGFOP, $4.90
Special Darjeeling FTGFOP, $10.50
Keemun FOP, $3.60
First Grade Keemun FTGFOP, $4.60
Kenya (Subukia) FOP, $4.20
Lapsang Souchong, $4.95
Yunnan FOP, $3.50
Special Yunnan FOP, $4.20
China Black FOP, $2.60
Panyang Congou, $3.25

Also Available: Herbals, flavored and decaffeinated teas, many new this year. Available in
both 21-bag package or in 2, 4 or 8 oz. packages.

Roger Virge (B)
(Available at many fine gourmet shops)

Rowley's of Ireland (B)
(Available at many fine English and Irish food
shops)

Royal Gardens Tea Company (B)
PO Box 2390
Fort Bragg, CA 95437
(707) 961-0263
Mail Order Catalog
First came their beautiful packaging, then came
awards, but, always, what counts for this
exceptional tea firm is fine tea. Even their tea
bags are the finest gauze filled with whole
leaves, not crushed fannings or dust. A wonderful line. The catalog also showcases great
accessories, tea samplers and gift baskets and
their Thanksgiving Coffee products.

Prices are listed by loose-leaf and 24 tea-
bag packages.

GREEN
Green Goddess, $6.25; $3.95/24 tea bags
Japanese Blessing, (Gyokuru and Lung
Ching), $12.50 loose only

BLACK
Darjeeling, $9.00/$5.75
Ceylon, $6.75/$3.95

SPECIALTY
Yin Hao Jasmine, $9.00/$5.75
Russian Caravan, $5.80/$3.95
Lychee, $5.75/$3.95

Boysenberry, $5.75/$3.95
Gooseberry, $5.75/$3.95
Earl Grey, $5.80/$3.95

Schapira and Company (R)
17 W. 10th St.
New York, NY 10011
(212) 675-3733

The brothers Schapira have been selling fine coffees and teas for several decades and their selection continues to grow and astound. An excellent all-around shop for fine teas and accessories. Try their Flower Cup Ceylon.

SCI Cuisine Internationale (W)
PO Box 659
Camarillo, CA 93011
(805) 482-0791
Fax (805) 484-7971

A line of more than 30 tea balls, infusers and pinch spoons, in stainless steel and in silver-plate; tea filters and teacup warmers. For the trade only.

The Sensuous Bean of Columbus Avenue, Inc. (R)
66 West 70th St.
New York, NY 10023
(212) 724-7725
(800) 238-6845

Frequently rated number one in the Zagat survey, this coffee and tea shop carries an exceptional line of gourmet teas of the world, and boxed, bagged and loose teas from famous blenders. All the following are priced per 4 oz. package.

GREEN
China Gunpowder, $3.80
China Jasmine with flowers, $3.80
Imperial Green, pan fired, $3.80
Sencha Fukuye, $4.60

BLACK
Bancha Hougi Cha, $4.80
Ceylon Ultima #1, $2.80
China Yunnan, $3.80
Choice Darjeeling Long, $3.60
Dimbula (Ceylon), $3.80
Formosa Oolong, $2.80
Golden Assam, $2.80
Keemun, $2.80
Kenya Michimukuru, $3.00
Lapsang Souchong, $2.80
Earl Grey/Lapsang, $3.50
Russian Style, $3.00
Sensuous Breakfast, $3.20

Also Available: Mate, herbal teas, flavored teas, decaffeinated teas and packaged teas, e.g., Bencheley, Bigelow Assorted Teas and Japan Green; Celestial Seasonings Herb Teas, Constant Comment, Eastern Shore, East India Teas and Stash Collections; Indar from France; Pompadour Herb Teas from Germany and Bewley's from Ireland; Fortnum & Mason, Jackson's of Piccadilly, Twinings and Ty-Phoo from England; and Hu-Kwa (Lapsang Souchong) from Taiwan.

Shamrock Irish Teas (B)
(Available at most fine English and Irish food and tea shops)

Silk Road Teas (O/W)
PO Box 287
Lagunitas, CA 94938
(415) 488-9017
Fax (415) 488-9015
Mail Order List
David Lee Hoffman is an importer of fine and rare teas, currently involved in a joint venture of a tea farm in Zhejiang province in China. An inveterate traveler, a textile expert, a worm farmer, a man who, literally and figuratively, wears many hats. He is a man passionate about China teas. His teas are served at some of Northern California's finest restaurants, health food shops and, of course, are available by mail order. Because his teas are very limited in quantity (often from a single farmer), they are in great demand; the list below, therefore, is a guideline only but a fair representation of the range (over 200) he offers. All the teas are personally chosen by Hoffman. Please inquire about currently available choices. All selections are 30 grams each, unless otherwise noted, and are $10 per bag; six bags for $50. Exact brewing instructions are included and sampler packs are available.

WHITE
Silver Needle
White Peony, 80 grams

GREEN
Dragon Well, 40 grams
Green Peony Rosette, 8 pcs.
Spring Bud Peony Rosette
Spring Spear Tip
Jade Spring
Mao Feng, 60 grams
Huangshan Mao Feng, 25 grams

OOLONG
Dahongpao, 20 grams
Dragon Ball, 3 pcs.
Dragon's Beard, 1 pc.
Fujian Oolong, 40 grams
Iron Goddess, 40 grams
Dai Bamboo, 50 grams
Phoenix Select

BLACK
Black Peony Rosette, 8 pcs.
Keemun with Rose, 80 grams
Pu-Erh, 80 grams
Yunnan Black, 100 grams
Liubao, 80 grams

**The Harrons of
Simpson & Vail Inc.** (O/W)
PO Box 309, 38 Clinton St.
Pleasantville, NY 10570
(914) 747-1336

(800) 282-TEAS
Fax (914) 741-6942
Mail Order Catalog

Quality teas and coffees since 1929. Prices are per pound, uness noted; smaller quantities upon request.

GREEN
Chunmee, $11.60
Dragon Well, $20.00
Gunpowder Imperial Green, $11.75
Pan-Fired Green Tea, $11.75
Young Hyson, $13.95
Banchar, $22.00
Genmaicha, $20.00
Kokeicha, $20.00
Gyokuro, $85.00 (1 oz. quantities which make 10–12 cups, $5.40)
Sencha, $25.00

The following are the latest additions of greens to the Simpson & Vail catalog; prices vary, so please call for quote (CFQ):
China Silver Sprout
Java Green
China Green Sencha
China Dong Yong Dong Bie
Darjeeling Green Resleehat

OOLONG
China Oolong, $11.95
Formosa Oolong, $11.95
Goddess of Mercy (Ti Kuan Yin), $21.00

Formosa Fancy Oolong, $75.00 (1 oz. quantities brew 10–12 cups, $4.80)
Formosa Oolong, $11.95

BLACK
Assam, $14.50
Ceylon Nadoototem, $13.75
Ceylon Orange Pekoe, $11.80
Ceylon Small Leaf, $9.25
China Keemun, $12.70
Darjeeling, $16.50
Darjeeling, Margaret's Hope Estate, Second Flush, $25.00
English Breakfast (Keemun), $14.00
Kenya/Marinyn, from Kericho District, $17.00
Lapsang Souchong, $17.95
Tippy Yunnan, $16.70

SPECIALTY TEAS
Morgan Blend, the original formula of Mr. Vail and J. P. Morgan, blended with Earl Grey, Lapsang Souchong and other strong teas, $14.25
Rose Congou, China black with fragrant rose petals, $11.25
Simpson & Vail Blend, combines Ceylon and Indian Teas, $13.75

Also Available: American Classic Tea; decaffeinated teas, aromatic and blended teas, flavored and decaffeinated flavored bulk; many tea-table food items, including Billington's Sugars; teacups, teapots, cosies and other paraphernalia, gift baskets.

Smith & Jamieson (B)
(See O'Mona International)

SPORTea (B)
Denver Tech Center
7340 S. Alton Way, Unit K
Englewood, CO 80112
(303) 694-6965
Fax (303) 694-7211
From climbers of Mt. Everest to local mountain bikers, everyone is looking for a refreshing drink, and iced tea is a typical choice. Although not a gourmet tea per se, it certainly has a black tea base, with Siberian ginseng and maté, an herb from South America. This is an ideal beverage to wean your family away from soda pop or yourself from coffee and diet drinks. Available at Hickory Farms nationwide and Whole Foods Markets in Texas, Illinois and California and many fine food shops. Twenty cup-size teabags, $4.95.

Stash Teas (B/W)
PO Box 910
Portland, OR 97207
(503) 684-4482
(800) 547-1514
Fax (503) 684-1514
Stash specializes in interesting traditional and iced tea blends, all available in their brightly-colored-foil–wrapped tea bags. However, Stash also has a very commendable list of traditional, loose-leaf teas, available in 2 and 6 oz. sizes or in 2 oz. sizes with an attractive canister. The following prices are for the 6 oz. size, which yields about 75–90 cups.

WHITE
Flowery Pekoe White, $30.00
Mutan White Tea, Special Grade, $19.00

GREEN
Dragonwell Special Grade, $20.00
Gunpowder Temple of Heaven, $9.00
Gyokuro Asahi (Pearl Dew), $15.00
Huo Mountain Yellow Sprouting, $17.50
Premium Green Tea in 30 tea bags, $4.45
Yamamotoyama Gen Mai Brown Rice Tea, 7 oz./$4.50
Traditional Green Tea, 3.5 oz./$4.50
Hoji-cha Roasted Green Tea, 3.5 oz./$4.50
Premium Special Occasion Green Tea, 3.5 oz./$6.00
Yamamotoyama Classic Oriental Teas: Green, Roasted, Brown Rice, Jasmine and Assam, each $3 for 16 tea bags

OOLONG
Formosa Oolong Fancy Grade, $15.00
Ti Kuan Yin Oolong, Special Grade "Goddess of Mercy," $15.00

BLACK
Assam Estate, Golden Tipped Leaves (TGFOP), $9.00
Ceylon Estate FOP, $9.00

Darjeeling Estate, Golden Tipped Leaves
(TGFOP), $15.00
Estate Breakfast, $15.00
Irish Breakfast , $7.50
Keemun, $7.50
Lapsang Souchong, $7.50

Also Available: Loose tea samplers, e.g., Green
Tea Treasures, three 2-oz. canisters, $24.00,
plus eight others; tea balls and infusers and
Swiss Gold Tea Filters, teapots, mugs, honey
sticks, and tea kettles; iced, decaffeinated teas,
herbals, spiced and flavored teas.

Susan's Teas (B/W)
(*See* First Colony Teas)

Sushi Chef (B)
Baycliff Company, Inc.
242 E. 72nd St.
New York, NY 10021
(212) 772-6078
Fax (212) 472-8980
Sushi Chef Japanese Green Tea, 1.9 oz in 24
teabags, $2.59

Svadlena's Tea Specialties (O)
1842 W. Palm Dr.
Mt. Prospect, IL 60056
(708) 806-0738
Price sheet available. All prices are for 4 oz.
loose-leaf teas; may be ordered in 8 oz. sizes
for double the price.

GREEN
China Chun Me, $4.50
China Jasmine, $6.00

OOLONG
Oolong Silver Blossom, $18.50

BLACK
Assam Heeleakah FOP, $6.50
Darjeeling Himalaya, $9.00
South-Indian FOP, $6.50
Ceylon Bombagalla Pekoe, $4.50
Ceylon OP Dimbula, $5.50
Szechuan, Smoky China Tea, $5.00

Also Available: A 4-, 6- and 12-month Tea Subscription tea club; fruit teas, flavored black teas
with primarily Ceylon/China blends, herbal
teas, tea tins and tea accessories.

Swee-Touch-Nee Tea (B)
(Available in most supermarkets in the kosher
foods section)

Taylor's of London (B)
Pagoda House
Prospect Road
Harrogate, North Yorkshire
HG2 7NX
England, UK
(0423) 889822
Since 1886, Taylors of Harrogate has sold tea
and coffee throughout Great Britain, often

blending teas suited to the variations in local water. Yorkshire Tea, their most popular blend, is blended to suit different regions. Now all of the line is available here in the United States in tea bags, loose tea and a variety of packaging with selections of green, black and blended teas, and scented teas available in bags and loose leaf. Available at most specialty and English tea/gift shops. Voted best tea in England.

Tea for Me (B)
(*See* Alexander Gourmet Imports, Ltd.)

Tea Garden Springs (O/R)
A spa for nurturing body, mind and soul
38 Miller Ave.
Mill Valley, CA 94941
(415) 389-7123
Fax (415) 389-7107

Jacqueline Sa has combined the calming, healing qualities of the tea experience with the equally nourishing qualities of a health spa that combines Chinese herbalism, aromatherapy, healing waters and a restful tea garden. Open ten A.M. to seven P.M., Tuesday through Saturday; Sundays from twelve to six P.M.

Teas by the pot or to purchase: Mutan White Tea (White Peony), $2.00 per oz.; Ti Kuan Yin Oolong, $4.50 per oz., Yin Hai Jasmine Scented Green Tea, $5.30 per oz., Gu Jian Mao Jian Green Tea, $4.20 per oz. and Erh Mee Mao Feng, Green Tea, $7.70 per oz.,

plus many other varieties available during their seasons, imported directly from China.

Tea Masters of London (B)
(*See* Alexander Gourmet Imports, Ltd.)

Tea to You, Inc. (O)
3712 N. Broadway, Box 471
Chicago, IL 60613
(800) 832-8696
Fax (312) 871-6987

Custom-designed tea baskets are available for $29.99, or try their monthly tea club membership for 3, 6 or 12 months for $12.95 per month. Company specializes in both gourmet blends, herbal decafs and a special Green Tea program for teas in either your choice of loose or bagged. Corporate memberships also available.

Teaneck Tea (B)
(*See* Harney & Sons)

Teahouse Kuan Yin (R)
1911 N. 45th St.
Seattle WA, 98103
(206) 632-2055
and
Mail Order/Wholesale (W/R)
1707 N. 45th St.
Seattle, WA 98103
(206) 632-2056
Fax (206) 632-8689
Tea List

When Teahouse Kuan Yin "fired up its tea kettles" in 1990, they aimed to establish a quiet oasis for the tea drinker who wanted the finest, freshest teas in a fusion of Asian and English styles enhanced by delicious food and live music. To ensure these pleasures, the wholesale and mail order department was developed and now serves the Wallingford District teahouse and many natural food stores, restaurants, cafes, gourmet food shops and other quality-conscious tea buyers. All prices below are for 8 oz.; minimum order is usually 2 oz.

WHITE
Shou-Mei, $23.00

GREEN
Longjing: Sparrow's Tongue, $9.95
Pearl Brow, $6.15
Green Peony, $36.00 (for 50)
Jasmine, $10.25
Yin Hao, $17.90
Formosa Jade, $21.50
Sencha, $28.00
Genmaicha, $14.50
Hojicha, $14.35
Willowleaf Bancha, $14.35
Matcha: Shohaku, $26.00/ 40-gram tin

OOLONG
Bao Jong, $22.75
Tung Ting: Winter Pick, $21.25

Bai Hao, $23.25
Ti Kuan Yin: Special, $36.00

BLACK
Darjeeling (Chamong Garden), $11.75
Darjeeling (Goomtee Estate), $11.25
Assam (Rembeng Estate), $11.75
Nilgiri (Burnside Estate), $7.50
Ceylon (Brunswick Estate), $7.50
Cameronian, $7.50
West Java, $7.50
Keemun, $7.60
Yunnan, $7.60
Lapsang Souchong, $7.65
Earl Grey, $8.00

Also Available: Pu-Erh (10 years old), $17.15; Herbal Tisanes: Haiku, Wu-Wei, World Peace, Taiwan Chrysanthemum, Chamomile, Organic Peppermint, $9.25 to $21.00.

Teeccino
Four flavored teas created to emulate flavored cappuccinos.
(*See* Victoria's Treasure)

Ten Ren Tea and Ginseng Company, Inc. (R)
75 Mott St., New York, NY 10013
(212) 349-2286
(800) 292-2049
Fax (212) 349-2180

and
135-18 Roosevelt Ave.
Flushing N.Y. 11354
(718) 461-9305
(Other locations in Monterey Park and
San Francisco, CA, and in Chicago)
This world wide marketer of fine Taiwan (Formosa) oolongs and other teas is an excellent place to sample teas Chinese-style. For more than forty years, this tea company with more than ten stores outside of Taiwan offers 120 grades of more than thirty different teas, but their specialty is Formosa Oolongs. Sizes of choices below vary because of leaf size.

WHITE
Shou Mei, $12.60
Shui Sheng, $12.60

GREEN
Gunpowder, $7.00
Jasmine, $62.60 to $7.20
Long Gin, $50.00 to $12.60
Green Oolong, $118.80 to $12.60
Pouchong Green, $93.80 to $7.20
Ginseng Oolong King's Tea (Green), $130.68 to $43.56

OOLONG
Dark Oolong, $89.10 to $7.60
Ti Kuan Yin, $89.10 to $7.80
Osmanthus Oolong, $118.80 to $35.60

Ginseng Oolong King's Tea (Dark), $21.80 to $87.20
Tung-Ting Oolong, varies

BLACK
Lapsang Souchong, $10.80
Lychee, $7.00
Oriental Beauty (Chamagne), $33.00

SPECIALTY TEAS
Puerh, $93.80 to $7.20
Puerh, First grade to Sixth grade, $118.80 to $9.80
Ten-Wu, $29.05 to $116.20
Ten-Lu, $29.05 to $116.20

Also Available: Many varieties of packaged teas, tea-bag tea, traditional, flavored, scented and herbal, and their famous Diet Tea; tea candies; Barley tea, Chrysanthemum teas; Ginseng teas; fine Yu-xing teapots and cups and related Chinese-style tea accessories, tea caddies and other paraphernalia.

Treasure Teas (B)
(*See* Windward Trading)

T Salon and Tea Emporium
142 Mercer St.
New York, N.Y. 10012
(212) 925-3700
(800) NYC TEAS
Fax (212) 343-2287

Miriam Novalle, a former "nose" in the perfume industry, has brought her senses to bear in creating her own line of blended and scented teas at her salon—in addition to the more than 200 varieties available for you to savor with your afternoon tea menu or to take home and enjoy. T Salon Teas are available by mail order through the salon and in certain other shops.

Twinings (B)
(Available at most major supermarkets and specialty food stores)

Ty-Phoo (B)
(Available at most fine English and Irish food shops; *see* Dean & Deluca)

Upton Tea Imports (MO)
231 South Street
Hopkinton, MA 01748
(800) 234-TEAS
Quarterly newsletter/price list
Tom Eck established this exemplary mail-order company in 1989 and is already selling almost one ton of tea per month. His extensive catalog presently lists about 120 teas from around the world, most of considerable distinction. Chatsford teapots, too.

All the following prices are for 125 grams, unless otherwise noted.

WHITE TEAS
First Grade Sgiy Neu Wgute Tea (Fujian), $3.90, 60g
Special Grade Mutan White, $4.90, 60g
China Yin Zhen Bai Hae Downy White Pekoe, $22.00, 60g

GREEN TEAS
Tian-Mu Qing Ding, $7.80, 80g
Pi Lo Chun (China Green Snail Spring), $18.60, 100g
Pan-Long-Ying Hao (Superfine), $12.40, 100g
Yu-Hua (Flower Rains) Green, $10.80, 100g
Long-Jing (Dragonwell) Superfine, $11.00, 100g
Young Hyson, $3.40
Chunmee, $3.80
First Grade Gunpowder Green, $3.60
Special Grade Temple of Heaven Gunpowder Green, $4.50
Yunnan Green (Silvertip), $4.40
Pi Lo Chun (Formosa), $8.80, 100g
Japanese Sencha, $5.90
Japanese Sencha Special Grade, $8.60
Gen-mai Cha, $4.80, 100g
Ko-kei Cha, $4.60
Ho-ji Chaa (Bancha), $2.80, 50g
Japanese Cherry (Bancha with cherry), $4.90
Gyokuro, $15.80
Matcha (Powdered Gyokuro for Japanese Tea Ceremony), $19.80, 40g tin

OOLONGS (FORMOSA)
Oolong Fine Grade, $4.50, 100g
Oolong Finest Grade, $6.00, 100g
Oolong Fancy, $10.50, 100g
Oolong Silvertip, $10.50, 80g
Oolong Silvertip (Top Superior), $12.80, 80g
Imperial Oolong, $12.80, 60g

OOLONGS (CHINA)
China Oolong Blend, $4.90, 100g
Tie-Guan-Yin Oolong First Grade, 100g
Tie-Guan-Yin Oolong Special Grade, $8.80, 100g

BLACK
Orthodox TGFOP Darjeeling, $5.20
No.1 Tippy Orthodox GFOP Darjeeling, $7.50
Makaibari Estate BOP Darjeeling, $4.60
Teesta Valley Estate FTGFOP1 Darjeeling, $6.60
Ambootia Estate FTGFOP1, $7.80
Risheehat Second Flush FTGFOP1, $6.60
Risheehat Green Darjeeling, $7.80
Castleton Estate Second Flush FTGFOP1, $25.00
Singulli Estate Autumnal FTGFOP1, $7.50
Makaibari Second Flush FTGFOP1(S/CL), $8.80
Milling Hills Estate FTGFOP1, First Flush, $6.80
Namring Estate FTGFOP1, First Flush, $10.60

Namring (Upper) Second Flush, $14.20
Namring (Upper) FTGFOP1, Second Flush, $23.00
Margaret's Hope Estate FTGFOP1 Second Flush, $7.80
Puttabong Estate FTGFOP1, First Flush, $16.80
Puttabong Estate Silver Tip, $8.20
Phuguri Estate Second Flush Darjeeling FTGFOP1, $12.50
Selimbon Second Flush Darjeeling FTGFOP1, $19.80
Moondakotee Second Flush, $8.80
Seeyok Estate Second Flush, $12.80
Darjeeling samplers of 50g of four choices each of 50 grams each, $22.00 and $34.50
Assam Tippy Orthodox GFOP, $4.90
CTC Fine Assam, $3.90
Toonabarrie Estate First Flush Assam, $4.60
Anandabag Estate Assam FTGFOP, $5.60
Mangalam Estate TGFOP1, Lot 767, $9.20/100g
Mangalam Estate TGFOP1, Lot 761, $46.60/100g
Joonktollee Estate Assam FTGFOP1, $3.90
Doomni Estate FSFTGFOP, $9.80/100g
Halmari Estate GT/GFBOP, $7.80/100g
Towkok Estate Assam SFTGFOP, $9.40/100g
Broken Leaf Assam Teas from various estates, priced $3.60 to $9.80 for 100–125g
Nilgiri BOP, $3.90
Mayfield Estate Bold Brokens OP, $2.80/100g
Tiger Hill Estate Flowery OP, $3.60/100g

Sikkim TGFOP (Temi Estate), Standard, $6.90
Sikkim TGFOP (Temi Estate), Superior, $9.40
Golden Nepal Kanyam Estate, $5.50
Special Nepal SFTGFOP (Kanyam Estate), $6.80
Special Nepal SFTGFOP (Malroom Estate), $8.40
Ceylon BOOP, $2.90
Dimbula BOP, $4.20
Kandy BOP, $4.00
Nuwara Eliya BOP, $4.30
Uva BOP, $4.20
Orthodox Process Orange Pekoe (Pettigalla Estate), $3.90, 100g
Orthodox Process Orange Pekoe (Kenilworth Estate), $3.90, 100g
Orthodox Process Fancy Orange Pekoe, Devonia Estate, $5.40, 100g
Chelsea Estate BOP, $5.60
China Black FOP, $2.50
China Cougou Pan Yang, $3.90
China Keemun, $4.00
China Keemun First Grade, $5.90
Hubei Province Keemun Ji Hong, $6.00
Hao-Ya ôBö Superfine Keemun, $8.70
Sichuan Zao Bei Jian, $8.40
China Keemun Mao Feng, $9.80, 100g
China Congou Ning Hong Jing Hao, $11.00
Yunnan GFOP, $4.20
Yunnan TGFOP, $6.10

Rare Grade Royal Yunnan, $18.00
Lapsang Souchong, $4.00, 100g
Lapsang Souchong Imperial, $4.40, 100g
Kenya GFBOP1, $3.90
Kenya GFBOP1 (Finest), $4.60
Golden Kenya TGFOP, $4.60

Also Available: Decaffeinated teas, Tea Bricks, Fruit and Flavored Teas, Jumbo Packets and Bags, suitable for 220 to 440 cups of tea, five Breakfast blends, four Earl Grey Bends, six Afternoon Tea blends and six Scented Teas.

Victoria's Treasure/Tea 2000 (B/W)
Towers 101
9930 Pioneer Blvd.
Santa Fe Springs, CA 90670
(800) 4488-TEA

The elegant black and gold tins of Victoria's Treasure offers loose tea in classic blends, e.g., English Breakfast, Irish Breakfast, Jasmine and Pure Ceylon, plus fruited black teas made with excellent flavorings: Mango, Blackberry, Apricot, Black Currant, Raspberry and Strawberry. They also carry five fruited iced-tea bags in upright wooden chest. Suggested retail $4.99 to $5.99 for tins; $2.99 to $3.99 for iced-tea bags. Sold at fine gourmet and upscale food markets everywhere.

Also Available: Jacksons of Picadilly, Fortnum & Mason, Ty-Phoo, Kenya Classique, Twinings, Xanadu, Teeccino.

John Wagner & Sons Inc. (B)
900 Jacksonville Rd.
BNC—5013
Ivyland, PA 18974
(215) 674-5000
Fax (215) 674-0398

From a small shop on Philadelphia's Dock Street, founded by John Wagner in 1847, this company has grown into one of the largest purveyors to the gift trade. The Wagner Museum, adjacent to their headquarters, sports many memorabilia about tea clipper travels and tea history. Admission is free.

All the following are packaged 24 teabags to the box and retail for approximately $3.00.

Imperial Green
Assam
Darjeeling
English Breakfast
Russian Caravan
Rare Mandarin (a blend of rare Black China teas and Orange Pekoe)
Irish Breakfast
Earl Grey
Ch'a Ching, a Chinese restaurant blend of Keemun, Oolong and Jasmine
Jasmine
Orange Pekoe
Keemun
Iced Tea Blend (Ceylon and South American teas)

Also Available: New line of Island Pleasure Tropic Teas, eight herb teas; six fruit teas; decaffeinated teas; tea gift sets; miniature and standard tea tins.

Wedgwood (B)

The maker of fine Jasper stoneware and and other ceramics has now launched a line of tea blends, created for them by England's Williamson & Magor. The teas are available in 4.4 oz. classically designed caddies in Wedgwood Blue for $7.00 and packages of 25 foil-wrapped sachets for $4.00. The following blends and selections are currently available in the U.S.: Pure Ceylon, Pure Darjeeling, Pure Uva, Wedgwood Original, Nuwara Eliya, Pure Assam, China Black, Orange Pekoe, English Rose, English Apple, English Breakfast and Earl Grey. All are excellent full-bodied teas and a good addition to the packaged tea market. Available at most upscale markets.

Mark T. Wendell Importer (O)
PO Box 1312
West Concord, MA 01742
(508) 369-3709
Fax (508) 369-7972
Mail Order Catalog

Since 1904, when Mark T. Wendell changed the name of his uncle's flagship tea from XXX to Hu-Kwa, in honor of the Chinese merchant Houqua, with whom his uncle traded, millions of people have enjoyed this distinctive smoky tea. In 1971 new owner Elliot H. Johnson expanded the 5-tea list (Hu-Kwa, Cheericup, M. T. W. Keemun, Jasmine and Formosa Oolong) to 35 exceptional teas and some packaged teas, including the Boston Harbour Tea. All prices are for 1/2 lb. quantities, except where noted.

WHITE
China White, $12.95/5 oz.

GREEN
Yin Hao Jasmine, $21.00
Lung Ching (DragonWell), First Grade, $90.00/500 grams (17.5 oz.)
Young Hyson, $10.25
Gunpowder, $9.95
Sencha of Shizuoka region, $13.50

OOLONG
Extra Fancy Formosa Oolong, $36.00
Formosa Oolong, $10.95
China Oolong, $10.95

BLACK
Extra Fancy First Flush Darjeeling, $18.00
English Breakfast, $9.75
Earl Grey, $10.95
Indonesian, $9.95
Mountain Kenya, $10.75
China Lapsang Souchong, $11.25
Russian Caravan, $9.95
M.T.W. Keemun, from Formosa, $10.50

Cheericup Ceylon, $8.25
Darjeeling, $12.50
China Yunnan, $10.75
China Keemun, $10.75
Irish Breakfast, $10.25
Assam, $10.25
China Panyong, $9.95

SPECIALTY
Hu-Kwa, $11.25, or 14 oz. tin, $15.75

Also Available: Ten Tea Sampler; flavored teas; M.T. Wendell's Gift Sampler.
Packaged teas from Lifeboat Tea, Boston Harbour Tea, Sushi Chef Japanese Green, Melrose's, P.G. Tips, Ty-Phoo and Indar.

Williamson & Magor (B)
(*See* Camellia Tea Company)

Windward Trading Company (W)
PO Box 9833
San Rafael, CA 94912
(800) 858-8119
(415) 457-2411
Fax (415) 457-4916
This wholesale company offers a range of tea balls, tea infusers, teapots, canisters, mugs and teapots, along with two proprietary blends of teas: Treasure Tea is sold in 100-gram packages of loose tea. Six flavored teas along with such traditionals as English Breakfast, Earl Grey and Queen's Own Choice. They also carry "Wind-

ward Trading Company Teas," as follows, which are wholesaled to coffee and tea shops and other specialty food and gourmet stores:

GREEN
China Gunpowder
Japanese Sencha

OOLONG
Famous Fine Oolong
Fancy Black Dragon Oolong

BLACK
Assam BOP
Ceylon BOP Highgrown
Ceylon OP Highgrown
Darjeeling TGFOP Spring
Darjeeling FOP Autumnal
China Golden Yunnan
China Keemun Black
Golden Nepal Tea
Malty Assam

SPECIALTY TEAS
China Jasmine
China Lapsang Souchong
English Earl Grey
Russian Caravan
Russian (Georgian)
English Breakfast

Also Available: Six decaffeinated and 14 blended black teas, tea-table paraphernalia including teapots, mugs, covered cups, caddies, cosies, strainers and filters.

Xanadu (B/W)
This line of teas from CBI (Coffee Bean International) is fast becoming the premier packaged tea brand in gourmet food shops. You can order them directly from the following mail order source or from Victoria's Treasure:

Coffee People (R)
Mail Order Dept.
4130 S.W. 117th Ave.
Beaverton, OR 97005
(503) 643-3053

Price is generally $6.75 for each 4 oz. package of loose-leaf tea. Two-pound minimum for all special orders.

GREEN
Genmaicha
Sencha Spiderleg
Young Hyson
Zhejiang Dragonwell
Pan Fired Green

OOLONG
Black Dragon Oolong
Fanciest Oolong

BLACK
Ceylon Kenilworth Highlands Estate

Star of Persia
Nakury Golden Peak
Darjeeling Lingla Estate
India Assam Estate
Madagascar
Night Bloom Jasmine
Lapsang Souchong
China Anhui
China Zhejiang
India Darjeeling TGBOP
China Temple of Heaven
Golden Nepal FTGFOP

Also Available: Flavored teas such as Black Cassis, Maharani Passion Fruit, Thai Lemon, Harmony Garden, Tropical Breeze, Emperor's Apple, Po Lin Peach, Market Spice, and classic blends such as Russian Caravan, Earl Grey, English or Irish Breakfast, and blends, e.g., Khan's Delight, Monk's Prayer and Himalayan Straw.

Yamamoto of the Orient (B)
(*See* O'Mona International)

Yorkshire Teas (B)
(*See* MacNab's Tearoom)

RECOMMENDED READING

PUBLICATIONS ON TEA

Gourmet Retailer
Michael Keighley, Editor
3301 Ponce De Leon Blvd.,
Suite 300
Coral Gables, FL 33134
(305) 446-3388
Free to Retailers

The Sage Report
1928 8th Ave W.
Seattle, WA 98119
(206) 282-1789
Publishes industry report, "U.S. Tea is 'Hot' Report," a market analysis resource for business & finance packaging. $175.00

Tea & Coffee Trade Journal
Jane Phillips McCabe, Editor
130 W. 42nd Street
New York, NY 10036
(212) 391-2060

Ukers' International Tea & Coffee Buyers Guide. (Produced by *Tea & Coffee Trade Journal;* see above)

The Tea Digest
Tea Council of Canada
701 Evans Avenue, Suite 501
Etobicoke, Ontario
Canada M9C1A3

Tea Talk, a newsletter on the pleasures of tea
Diana Rosen, Editor
PO Box 860
Sausalito, CA 94966
(415) 331-1557

World Coffee and Tea Magazine
McKeana Publications, Inc.
636 First Ave.
West Haven, CT
(203) 934-5288

THE BEST BOOKS ON TEA

Blofield, John. *The Chinese Art of Tea.* Boston: Shambala Publications, 1985.

Bromah, Edward. *Tea and Coffee: A Modern View of 300 Years of Tradition.* Arizona: G. F. Hutchinson Press, 1972.

Chow, Kit with Kramer, Ione. *All the Tea in China.* California: China Books and Periodicals, Inc., 1990.

Etherington, Dan and Forster, Keith. *Greengold: The Political Economy of China's Post-1949 Tea Industry.* New York: Oxford University Press, 1994.

Evans, John C. *Tea in China: The History of China's National Drink.* Connecticut: Greenwood Publishing Group Inc., 1992.

Fortune, Robert. *A Visit to the Tea Districts of China.* Vermont: John Murray, 1852.

Goodwin, Jason. *A Time for Tea: Travels Through China and India in Search of Tea.* New York: Alfred A. Knopf Inc., 1991.

Hammitzsch, Horst. *Zen in the Art of the Tea Ceremony.* New York: Penguin Books, 1972.

Hobhouse, Henry. *Seeds of Change: Five Plants That Transformed Mankind.* New York: Harper & Row, 1986.

Israel, Andrea. *Taking Tea: The Essential Guide to Brewing, Tasting and Entertaining With Tea.* New York: Grove/Atlantic Inc., 1987.

The Illustrated Tea Address Book. New York: Exley Publications Ltd., 1989.

Kakuzo, Okakura. *The Book of Tea.* Boston: Charles E. Tuttle Co.,1956. Several versions have also been published by Dover, Random House, Farrar Strauss, and Shambhala Publications.

McCormick, Malachai. *A Decent Cup of Tea.* New York: Clarkson Potter Publishers, 1991.

McCoy, Elin and Walker, John Frederick. *Coffee and Tea: The Complete Guide to Evaluating, Buying, Preparing, and Enjoying Every Variety of Coffee and Tea,* 3rd ed. New York: Raines & Raines, 1993.

Pettigrew, Jane. *Time for Tea: A Book of Days.* New York: Little, Brown and Company, 1991.

Pratt, James Norwood. *The Tea Lover's Treasury.* California: Cole Publishing Group, 1994.

Repplier, Agnes. *To Think of Tea!* London, U.K.: Jonathan Cape Ltd., 1933.

Sadler, A.L. *Chan-o-yu.* Boston: Charles E. Tuttle Company, 1962.

Seer, Highland, with an introduction by Pratt, James Norwood. *Reading Tea Leaves.* New York: Clarkson Potter Publishers, 1994.

Sen, Soshitsu. *Tea Life, Tea Mind.* New York: Weatherhill Inc., 1979.

Simpson, Helen. *The London Ritz Book of Afternoon Tea: The Art and Pleasures of Taking Tea.* New York: Arbor House, 1986.

Smith, Michael. *The Afternoon Tea Book.* New York: Atheneum, 1989.

Stella, Alain, Brochard, Gilles, Beautheae, Nadine, and Donzel, Catherine with a foreward by Burgess, Anthony. *The Book of Tea.* New York: Abbeville Press, 1992.

Thomas, Senlo. *The Tea Ceremony.* New York: Harmony Books, 1978.

Varley, Paul and Isao, Kumakua. *Tea in Japan: Essays on the History of Chanoyu.* Hawaii: University of Hawaii Press., 1979.

Versten, Ian. *Coffee Floats, Tea Sinks: Through History and Technology to a Complete Understanding.* Tulsa, Ok.: Helien Publishing, 1993.

Ukers, William H. *All About Tea.* New York: Tea and Coffee Trade Journal Company, 1935.

Yu, Lu, interpreted and translated by Carpenter, Francis R. *Cha's Ching.* New Jersey: Ecco Press, 1995.

_____.*The Classic of Tea.* New York: Little, Brown and Company, 1974.

GLOSSARY OF TEA-TASTING TERMS

Agony of the leaves: Unfolding of the leaves in boiling water

Aroma: Also known as nose or fragrance, it is actually the odor of both the infused leaf and the tea liquor itself. Most analogies are to flowery essences or fruits, e.g., a peachlike smell to some oolongs.

Astringency: That quality of the liquor that gives a bite, or puckeryness, to the liquor

Baggy: A residue or stain that results from unlined hessian bags

Bakey: Unpleasant taste caused by firing leaf at too high a temperature and removing too much moisture; not as strong as "burnt"

Biscuity: Pleasant characteristic often associated with Assam teas

Bite: Not a taste but the astringent puckeriness that gives black tea its refreshing quality

Bitter: An unpleasant biting taste, frequently resulting from oversteeping or allowing teas to remain too long in the liquor

Black: A dark brownish-black appearance of the leaf, a desirable characteristic of a fully fermented leaf

Blackish: Typical of carefully sorted CTC (cut-tear-curl) tea leaves; refers to leaf's appearance

Bloom: Sheen or luster on black leaf as a result of minimal handling and sorting

Body: Viscosity, the strength of the liquor combined with its weight on the tongue; body may be "full," "light," etc.

Bold: Large leaf or sometimes pieces of leaf too big for a grade, outsized

Brassy: Unpleasant tang or brasslike metallic taste caused by underwithering

Bright: Sparkling liquor characteristic of all fine teas; also describes taste opposite of "dull"

Brisk: Lively, not flat, and a true characteristic of well-manufactured teas

Brown: An indication of overly harsh treatment of CTC-type teas; a brown appearance

Burnt: Extreme overfiring

Character: An attractive taste quality of high-grown teas

Chesty: Resinous odor or taste imparted by uncured wood or inferior packing materials in a tea chest

Chunky: A very large albeit broken-leaf tea

Clean: Tea leaf that is free of extraneous matter, particularly fiber, dust, twigs or similar particles

Coarse: Harsh taste; quite undesirable

Colory: Depth of color and strength

Common: A very indistinctly flavored liquor that is thin, light, plain, lacking in color or body; or, in reference to tea leaf, poor quality

Complex: The harmonious mélange of various flavors characteristic of the very finest teas

Creaming up: The occasional bubbly residue that comes to the surface of some black teas, especially Assams, harmless, and indeed desirable.

Creepy: Typical characteristic of O.P. teas which are larger-grade and broken-leaf teas; a crimped, creepy appearance

CTC (Cut, Tear, Curl): A process of tea which is done by machine and results in tea leaves which are cut but still very full of flavor.

Curly: Different than wiry (see below), this refers to the appearance of a whole-leaf grade of teas, i.e., O.P.

Dry: Over fired, but not burnt

Dull: Leaf without sheen, i.e., "bloom"

Earthy: Used to describe an earthy flavor which can be either natural from the region where the tea is grown or the result of storage in too damp an area

Empty: A tea characteristic of liquor without substance, fullness, body

Even: A grade of tea that has leaves which are uniformly even or nearly even in size

Flaky: Poorly made leaf that is flat, open and easily broken; nonpejoratively, small grades

Flat: Soft, rather flabby-bodied tea lacking "bite" and "briskness"

Flavor: Relatively rare but always sought after, usually most evident in teas of slow growth at high elevations

Fruity: Piquant quality characteristic of good oolongs, some Keemuns, etc.

Gone off: Tea that's been spoiled by improper storage or packing or is simply past its prime and is stale

Grainy: Primary grades of well-made CTC teas

Gray: Color caused by too much abrasion during the sorting process

Green: Refers to underfermentation of black tea or else leaves from immature bushes whose liquor often is raw or light; can also be caused by poor rolling; (not to be confused with greenish teas, first flush tea or with green tea properly so called)

Hard: Very pungent brew

Harsh: Very rough-tasting, underwithered tea

Heavy: Thick, strong, colory liquor with limited briskness to its taste

Lacking: A liquor without body, one that is neutral or without any strong characteristics

Leafy: Those teas whose leaves are large or long in size

Light: "Flaky," but also a tea that is light in weight and lacking density

Make: Well-made tea true to its grade; also poorly-made tea true to its grade

Malty: A subtle underlying flavor often characteristic of Assam

Mature: Not flat or bitter

Metallic: A sharp coppery taste

Muddy: Dull or opaque liquor without lightness

Muscatel: A muscat-grape-like taste used to characterize the finest Darjeelings

Mushy: Tea with a high moisture content as a result of its packaging or storage
Musty: Moldy smell or taste resulting from poor storage or packing; or mildew-affected tea; (not a defect in Pu-Er!)
Neat: A grade of tea with a good make and size
Nose: Aroma or smell of the dry leaf
Orange pekoe: Refers to the larger of the two leaves of a tea plant; the orange refers to the orangish or golden color of the leaf when plucked. As a tea blend, however, orange pekoe is a misnomer but has come to mean a pleasant everyday tea.
Ordinaire: A term, patterned after that of the wine industry, to describe a good, predictable tea suitable for daily drinking; ordinary table tea.
Pekoe: From the Chinese word pa-ko, or "white down," to describe the wispy hairs found on fine leaves. Tea has a leaf bud and two larger leaves; the largest of these two leaves is referred to as pekoe. Pekoe tea, however, is actually a misnomer and used for a common blend of pleasant but undistinctive taste.
Peak: The high point of tasting experience when, some instants after the liquor enters the mouth, its body, flavor and astringency make themselves fully felt. Greens and oolongs do not peak, but stand immediately and fully revealed.
Plain: A brew that is clean tasting but without major characteristics to make it lively
Pointy: A liquor is said to "have point" if it shows some desirable property—for example, briskness or fine fragrance
Powdery: Fine light tea dust
Pungent: Astringent; what gives a tea its bite; good combination of strength, brightness and briskness
Quality: Used to describe the cup of liquor's most wanted characteristics
Ragged: Badly manufactured and graded tea that is uneven
Self-drinking: Any tea with sufficient aroma, flavor, body and color to stand alone and in no need of blending for improvement
Shotty: Well-made Gunpowder green tea; sometimes also applied to black teas
Stalk and fiber: Plant residues which are generally included in lower-grade teas but should be at minimum in higher grade teas; reflects sloppy or indifferent sorting

Soft: The opposite of brisk; inefficient firing or fermentation causes this lack of liveliness

Stewed: Overstepped tea leaves which have turned bitter; also can refer to leaves that have been poorly fired at low temperatures and insufficient air flow, resulting in a brew with a bitter taste.

Strength: Substantive characteristic of a cup of tea

Sweaty: Poor tea with unpleasant taste

Taint: Flavor or taste in tea that is foreign, i.e., oil, food, etc., that results from being stored next to such foods or products

Tarry: An aroma of smokiness associated with Lapsang Souchang or some Russian Caravan–style teas; scent derives from being smoked over wood or charcoal. (If it smells like rubber do not buy it.)

Thick: Brew with rich color and taste and strength

Thin: Opposite of thick; lacking color, taste, and having a thin or light liquor. Lacking body or color or both

Tip: Literally the tip of the youngest leaves, which is a true sign of good picking

Tippy: Generous amount of white or golden tip, i.e. budding leaf

Uneven or mixed: Leaves which show various colors

Weedy: May be applied to thin, cabbagy black teas; nonpejoratively, a green tea may be called weedy if it has a not-unpleasant vegetative aroma and flavor, varying from simple herbaceousness to scents of new-mown hay

Well-twisted: Fully withered, leaf of whole-leaf grades which is tightly rolled lengthwise

Winey: Usually descriptive of a mellow quality fine Darjeelings or Keemuns acquire with six months to a year or more of age; more rarely used to describe overfermented tea

Woody: Same as weedy

About James
Norwood Pratt

by Diana Rosen

*I*n all my dealings with the public about tea, afternoon tea, and tea accoutrements, the three most common inquiries I get are, (1) Does tea have more caffeine than coffee?* (2) What's the difference between afternoon and high tea?** and (3) Who's James Norwood Pratt?

I discovered Norwood the way most people do, through his books *The Wine Bibber's Bible*, and *The Tea Lover's Treasury*. The latter I found on sale (be still my heart) in a tea shop in Laguna Beach, California, while cruising for tea news for another column in my newsletter. I read it immediately upon arriving home and was thrilled to find finally a book on tea that was as elegantly written, as fun to read and as truly, truly informative as this one.

A native of North Carolina, where his family's history dates back generations, Norwood is a gentleman of the South, properly educated at home during his youth and

---

*Yes and no: see our chapter on tea and health for a complete explanation.
**High tea is a hearty supper common to the north of England; afternoon tea is what we all like with those cucumber sandwiches, scones and sweets.

182

left to his own devices to travel extensively and be educated publicly at Chapel Hill. Wherever Norwood has gone, adventure seemed to be awaiting him, and his has been a life of full and early understanding that life is to be enjoyed and friends are one's greatest wealth.

His first substantial writing was as a wine enthusiast. He was one of the very first to champion educating one's palate about California wines, and his book remains a classic in the field. Looking for a more gentle beverage, Norwood rediscovered tea, remembering his days at Chapel Hill, where there was a cult of tea, young men and women rushing quite ignorant yet not unwilling to be tea snobs. It was here he first became fascinated with the exotic-sounding names of Assam and Darjeeling and first learned the differences between oolongs and black teas—a far cry from his virgin tea experiences, traditional iced tea garnished with a sprig of mint, if you please.

Living in San Francisco during the heady sixties, when wine and coffee reigned supreme (as they do to this day), Norwood ferreted out the city's century-old carriage-trade coffee and tea merchant, Freed Teller & Freed's, where he first bought his coffee, then tried their teas. Owner Augie Techeira, rather than be irked by this young man with the questions, instead welcomed Norwood into the realm of fine teas, leading him further and further down a path of enchantment. It was on this path of discovery that his agent found him savoring teas and ignoring pleas for another wine book. Frustrated that Norwood had abandoned wine for this "lowly" beverage, the agent exasperatingly said, "Well, then, write about tea but write me another book!" And that's precisely what he did, resulting in his beloved classic, *The Tea Lover's Treasury*.

You can well imagine my delight when Richard Sanders of Grace Tea Company suggested I give Norwood a call about inviting him to be a columnist for my publication. I dashed off a letter and quickly had a reply (it was yes!), and we began a reserved albeit friendly editor-writer relationship. Through phone calls, our friendship deepened so that when we first met, for tea under the stained glass dome of Neiman-Marcus/San Francisco, we immediately became fast friends.

Norwood and I have spent many wonderful afternoons that frequently segue into early evenings at his San Francisco pied-à-terre, where we have tea while looking out toward the Bay. He uses a Chatsford teapot with an infusion basket, which he offers for me to "nose." (I use a no-name Thailand delicate white teapot at my home, and let the teas agonize to their heart's content.)

He pours the amber gold into oversized older Losmonotov cups and saucers (I offer gold-rimmed white Rosenthal or beflowered Noritake fortuitously and skillfully collected from thrift shops, although that hardly negates their real value to me.)

As for the tea, I like Uwa, Temi estate, Grace's winey Keemun, and other hearty teas that say "Notice me," while Norwood often opts for exquisite Darjeelings and delicate China greens, and we both try whatever is newest and most recently available to these shores from anywhere in the world, comparing previous cups and adding new names to our list of all-time favorites (for now).

The conversation swims gently from eighteenth-century personages to Greek myths to Gothic Southern tales; from Buddhism to Western religions to gentle gossip about friends and, always, stories about tea, both historical and apocryphal. We're surrounded by beautiful paintings, our feet rest on softly worn Oriental carpets and everywhere you look are wonderful artifacts, from black Wedgwood Basaltware tea sets to bronze sculpture to a family heirloom clock that persists in breaking the reverie despite our studiously ignoring its gentle gongs for as long as we can.

Norwood and I have become mutually enthusiastic tea siblings constantly in pursuit of new experiences.

My touchstone cup was one sipped after an arduous day as a tourist in London (it's not easy having a good time, y'know). I stopped by the Ceylon Tea Centre (now defunct) at Leicester Square and tasted what was surely a nectar of the tea gods, buying all I could to take home with me. My next favorite experience was pleading for an appointment for a pedicure at Harrod's, surely the most accommodating place in the world, which can see to your needs literally from birth to death (they have both cribs and coffins).

They were deeply apologetic that they only had a small antechamber to place me in; nonetheless I was thrilled with my warm foot bath, pile of British fashion magazines and a promptly delivered pot of tea and biscuits. Who could ask for anything more?

Actually, tea enthusiasts always want more as a part of the utterly selfish chase for further pleasures. Throughout our directory you will find entire countries' assortments of teas to consider, from the mundane to the sublime, now more readily available at the growing number of tea retailers throughout the fifty states. Your exploration, like ours, will be rewarded with infinitely satisfying brews, all of them healthful and most quite delicious.

While I can hardly invite you all to tea with Norwood (or, should you be interested, tea in my humble abode), I can promise you that tea will enhance your life. As you share your best teas with emerging or established friends, the intimacy, pleasure, humor and warmth of such friendships is gently nourished by this simple combination of water and leaf.